Wounded Writers Ask: Am I Doing it Write?

Wounded Writers Ask: Am I Doing it Write?

S. Rebecca Leigh

SENSE PUBLISHERS
ROTTERDAM/BOSTON/TAIPEI

A C.I.P. record for this book is available from the Library of Congress.

ISBN: 978-94-6209-711-7 (paperback)
ISBN: 978-94-6209-712-4 (hardback)
ISBN: 978-94-6209-713-1 (e-book)

Published by: Sense Publishers,
P.O. Box 21858,
3001 AW Rotterdam,
The Netherlands
https://www.sensepublishers.com/

Printed on acid-free paper

All Rights Reserved © 2014 Sense Publishers

No part of this work may be reproduced, stored in a retrieval system, or transmitted in any form or by any means, electronic, mechanical, photocopying, microfilming, recording or otherwise, without written permission from the Publisher, with the exception of any material supplied specifically for the purpose of being entered and executed on a computer system, for exclusive use by the purchaser of the work.

To all writers, wounded and fearless, I dedicate these pages.
And to Nor.

TABLE OF CONTENTS

Acknowledgements	ix
Chapter 1 Core Stories	1
Chapter 2 Joyful Nonsense	47
Chapter 3 Aesthetic Gifts	75
Chapter 4 Word Craft	97
The Writing Promise	113
Word Well	114
Namaste For Writers	115

ACKNOWLEDGEMENTS

I Wish To Thank

My undergraduate student from the Fall 2010 semester for suggesting that I write this book in the first place. I vaguely remember her saying she wanted to buy it after graduation so that she could approach writing with confidence in her first year of teaching. I do not remember this student's name because the suggestion at the time did not seem significant to me. It would take six months after that course before I could articulate why: I am a wounded writer. As such, it never occurred to me that I could write a book much less a book on writing. "Of magic doors there is this: You do not see them even as you are passing through." Wherever you are student of mine that was some door. Thank you.

The students who contributed their writing so that readers could see the potential of these invitations to write.

Jennifer Prince for helping me think through the title of this book.

Jackie Kerchyk for naming Clip N Create in Chapter Three and Laurie Lavins for exploring "Aesthetic Gifts" with children who have special needs, showing the world that all children have aesthetic gifts.

Amber Dietz for photographing the cover art. Best. Photographer. Ever.

Peter Gouzouasis for suggesting Sense Publishers and for recommending that I read Shaun McNiff's *Trust the Process*, a book that quickly became a vital ally in this creative work.

Ron Cramer, my friend and colleague, who believed not just in this book but in me – right from the start. Every wounded writer needs a fearless writer in her corner.

My family and friends for their love and support and Penny, sweet Penny, who put up with the running joke: "We'll go to the dog park in a minute."

INTRODUCTION

"I frequently call myself a wounded writer. Even now in middle age, I can still hear my grade 11 teacher say, You'll never be a writer and I can still hear other teachers and professors declare that my writing was mediocre, awkward, incoherent, faulty, loose, and fragmented" (p. 1).

This opening line in Carl Leggo's (2002) *What is Good Writing? Grammar and My Grandmother* captures for me something familiar about writing and the teaching of writing. What teachers say to us about our writing can have lasting impressions on us as writers and how we view our writing. For Ralph Fletcher (1993), it was his kindergarten teacher's comment, "You've got sloppy penmanship and sloppy penmanship means a sloppy personality" (p.11) that stayed with him well into adulthood. At one point or another, we have all been on the receiving end of these kinds of stinging comments from teachers that Leggo and Fletcher describe. Though I do not believe all teachers intentionally trivialize students' writing pursuits or are always aware of the power of their words, these kinds of judgments on our writing and/or efforts to write can profoundly wound our writerly spirit. So, too, can being denied opportunities to write about topics that genuinely matter to us. And when given rare opportunities to choose our own writing topics, we sometimes floundered. "The problem is no one in school," explains Goldberg (1990) "gave us permission to write what really happened" (p. 54). Many of our writing experiences were not experiences at all; rather, they were prescribed, assigned, and forced writing routines. In this writing climate, we learned to write for others rather than ourselves; we communicated to one person, the teacher (Graves, 1976).

When our writerly spirit is crushed, we develop what I call *writer woundedness*, a state of being that prevents us from trusting ourselves as capable of writing something we can feel good about. There are two factors that contribute, I believe, to this state: teacher judgment on our writing; and teacher control over the writing process.

As wounded writers, we stop trusting our creative instincts. In fact, we suppress creativity altogether. We convince ourselves that being creative is wasteful. We believe we have nothing important to say. When we write, we often do so on the heels of someone else's ideas rather than our own. We expect to know what to say before we write it, telling ourselves that we cannot write until we have a plan in place. We expect brilliance in first draft writing and loathe ourselves when we read what we have written. We hate the way it sounds. We cringe at the time wasted on just one sentence and become easily discouraged by the unfairness of writing, for the effort we put in does not always match the outcome (e.g., How can this be terrible when I worked on it for hours?). We agonize over choosing the right words. We worry about what others think. We measure our work against others. We convince ourselves that imitation is stealing. In sum, we put enormous pressure on ourselves to perform each time we set pencil to paper, fingers to computer keys. As wounded writers, we do not quiet our inner censor but create and accept, instead, an internal story that there is a right way to write. This story is so powerful it feeds our self-doubt and oppresses our ideas and our voices. "Perfectionism," said author Anne Lamott (1994) "is the voice of the oppressor" (p. 28).

HOW THIS BOOK CAME TO BE

The writing engagements in this book are free-writes (Elbow, 1973) or quick-writes that I use in my teacher education courses where I invite students to experience writing as a tool for: activating prior knowledge on a particular topic; exploring and entertaining ideas; answering questions; recording experiences; revisiting memories; accessing and engaging the imagination; and experimenting with form and meaning.

My students asked me to write this book because the writing engagements in these four chapters got them writing (again). Certainly, it is not unusual for teacher candidates to feel some anxiety toward writing and the teaching of writing; however, for many of my students the anxiety is unmistakable if not remarkable. Semester after semester, I have dealt with groups of wounded writers stacked against years of ill-considered remarks from their grade school teachers about their writing. For some students, these recollections are not only word for word but oftentimes vivid. Some describe controlled writing environments that, years later, still bother them. Though they have chosen a profession in which they will teach others to write, many admit their dread in doing so. I attribute some of their reluctance to write because writing simply and directly, says Ravitch (1984), is tricky business; it requires "the writer to show his cards" (p.7). Writer woundedness makes students afraid of showing their cards. Which cards do I show? Which ones are valued? Which do I talk about? And how do I talk about them?

I attribute my students' growth as writers to the discussions we had about each prompt before we wrote, the openness of the prompts, the relevance some of the prompts had for students (e.g., writing about oneself), the aesthetic and creative approach to writing, and self as audience. While I generally dislike writing to the prompt and agree with Donald Graves (1993) who is noted for the 20/80 per cent rule to prompt and choice writing, I believe prompts serve a purpose in the writing classroom. Free-writes are invitations that can offer students not only direction but also facilitate focus in writing. The free-writes in this book are open and therefore offer students multiple directions in which to take their story ideas.

HOW THIS BOOK IS ORGANIZED

This book includes free-writes that I have collected over the years for their generative writing potential. I like them for several reasons. First, they are nonthreatening and informal. They emphasize making meaning over what looks and sounds correct or polished. Second, they explore a range of writing, from the serious to the silly. Finally, these writing engagements are fun. Joyful experiences with writing address and dismantle woundedness by awakening creative consciousness, which allows students to explore, discover, and articulate their written voices.

There are four chapters in this book. Chapter one titled "Core Stories" concerns writing that deals with the self. This first chapter is where students delve into their own life stories as a pathway toward understanding who they are and how they see themselves. The exploration of personal life stories is identity-building, where students can break down self-doubt and construct their own sense of self.

Chapter two titled "Joyful Nonsense" addresses list writing. The purpose of this second chapter is to infuse fun into writing and dismantle notions that writing has to be proper to be good. Author Stephen King (2000) said it best: "Language does not always have to wear a tie and lace-up shoes" (p.134). Nonsensical work has value.

Chapter three titled "Aesthetic Gifts" engages the aesthetic and calls on writers to be intuitive and spontaneous. In my experiences in working with reluctant writers, aesthetic approaches to writing are both healing and restorative and often motivate students to write. Access to the aesthetic provides an inherent need to make sense of experience (Eisner, 1985).

Chapter four titled "Word Craft" emphasizes craft in writing. This fourth chapter calls on writers to apply what they know about how language works to transform ideas and explore meaning.

These four chapters offer students short, meaningful writing engagements as a pathway toward healing woundedness. They: help students look inward to discover who they are; create enjoyment in writing; provide fertile ground for developing ideas (e.g., discover a new word to describe an idea) and discovering new ones (e.g., story titles, stories, characters). While not all creative pursuits will lead to publication, it is hoped that some of these engagements will offer students possibility and direction in their writing.

HOW TO USE THIS BOOK

The free-writes in this book are short, brief engagements that do not put a lot of demands on the writer. Even so, *Core Stories* may feel demanding for some students because it requires them to show their cards about themselves. For others, *Word Craft* may be the most demanding because it triggers "extended, revised, and polished writing" (Romano, 2003, p. 52). *Joyful Nonsense* and *Aesthetic Gifts* put the least amount of demand on the writer with their emphasis on list writing and the aesthetic, which is why I start with these. These chapters share a playful spirit. "Playful writing," explains Kittle (2008) "leads to a comfortable voice that is easy to read (p. 31). Developing comfort in writing is an important goal as students work toward *Core Stories* and *Word Craft*, the first and fourth chapters. *Core Stories* is first in the book for a reason because dismantling writer woundedness truly begins with the self. Therefore, I encourage as much writing from this chapter as possible.

INTRODUCTION

In each free-write, I ask students to locate a potential story idea because, like Kittle (2008), I believe that through messy thinking, uncensored writing, "good writing grows" (p. 31). I also place a Word Well at each student's table, a jar of words or what Wooldridge (1996) calls word-tickets. This well includes 10-15 neologisms, surnames, street names, unique word combinations, strong verbs, etc. Students draw from these wells one random word that they may use anywhere in their free-writes. Often, I find the word well provides a starting point for many writers. At the back of this book, there is a list of words to get teachers started.

This book is for teachers who know they want to write with their students but who feel burdened by their own writing histories such that they struggle with where or how to start. The free-writes in this book provided my students a starting point to begin a new writing history. The pursuit to heal old writing wounds is a valid one: Teachers who write better understand the writing process and can empathize with struggling writers (Atwell, 1998) and those who share their writing with their students and provide demonstrations of craft in writing can support students' understanding of how language works (Smith, 1994). Press on, write on, be fearless dear writers.

REFERENCES

Atwell, N. (1998). *In the middle: New understandings about writing, reading, and learning.* Portsmouth, NH: Heinemann.
Eisner, E. (1985). Aesthetic modes of knowing. In E. Eisner (Ed.), *Learning and teaching the ways of knowing.* University of Chicago Press.
Elbow, P. (1973). *Writing without teachers.* London: Oxford.
Fletcher, R. (1993). *What a writer needs.* Portsmouth, NH: Heinemann.
Goldberg, N. (1990). *Wild wind: Living the writer's life.* New York, NY: Bantam.
Graves, D. (1976). Let's get rid of the welfare mess in the teaching of writing. *Language Arts, 53*(6), 645–651.
Graves, D. (1993). *A fresh look at writing.* Portsmouth, NH: Heinemann.
King, S. (2000). *On writing: A memoir of the craft.* New York, NY: Scribner.
Kittle, P. (2008). *Write beside them: Risk, voice, and clarity in high school writing.* Portsmouth, NH: Heinemann.
Lamott, A. (1994). *Bird by bird.* New York, NY: Anchor.
Leggo, C. (2002). What is Good Writing? Grammar and My Grandmother. *Inkshed, 19*(3). Retrieved May 18, 2012, from http://www.stthomasu.ca/inkshed/mar02.htm
Ravitch, D. (1984). Reviving the craft of writing. *College Board Review, 132,* 4–8.
Romano, T. (2003). Writing with voice. *Voices from the Middle, 11*(2), 50–55.
Smith, F. (1994). *Writing and the writer.* Hillsdale, NJ: Erlbaum.
Wooldridge, S. (1996). *Poemcrazy: Freeing your life with words.* New York, NY: Three Rivers Press.

CHAPTER 1

CORE STORIES

LOVE DON'T MEAN

Eloise Greenfield's (1978) *Honey, I Love* is a collection of love poems. "Love Don't Mean" (p. 37) is a departure from more traditional love poems where love is often romanticized to the exclusion of other kinds of love. Written from a child's perspective, the writing is simple yet powerful. I like to share this poem with students because it demonstrates how poetry demands keen observation of the world. Greenfield identifies an everyday act (e.g., watching over someone) as loving, which makes the poem relatable and encourages students to think about what love means to them and to express those ideas in a free verse poem.

Before Writing

Begin a discussion with students on what they know about love. For example, what symbols or words do they associate with love? What kind of gestures do they consider as loving? What are some different kinds of love? And whom do they love? (e.g., family, pets, friends, and places). Ask students to describe a time in their lives where love felt lasting or fleeting. Finally, read "Love Don't Mean." Make a copy of these lines so that students can see them projected from a document camera.

>Love don't mean all that kissing
>Like on television
>Love means Daddy
>Saying keep your mama company
>   till I get back
>And me doing it

During Writing

Invite students to write their own poem of Love Don't Mean. They may also draw from an experience in their lives that felt loving. Encourage students to avoid clichés and strive, instead, for originality. Ask them to consider writing about everyday loving acts.

After Writing

Invite individual students to share what they have written. The teacher may also invite several students to read one line only (e.g., Love don't mean…) and share across the room.

CHAPTER 1

Sharing Student Writing

> Love don't mean sleeping together every night
> Like everyone says they do
> Love means
> Picking up your clothes
> and hanging them up
> Even when you're dead tired
> And just wanna go to sleep
>   -Bob

> Love don't mean perfect
> Like me smiling every moment
> Love means
> Being okay with differences,
> Communicating and really listening
> Even, and especially when, you want to shut me out
> Love means staying
>   -Whitney

> Love don't mean flowers and candlelight.
> Sometimes, love means pretending not to notice that I am still in my pajamas from the night before and letting wine and grilled cheese pass for dinner. Love is letting me sleep in on Saturdays and reminding me that we are in this together.
>   -Martin

REFERENCE

Greenfield, E. (1978). *Honey, I love*. New York, NY. Harper.

CORE STORIES

WHERE I AM FROM

Linda Christensen's (2000) *Reading, Writing, and Rising Up: Teaching about Social Justice and the Power of the Written Word* provides a collection of ideas on how to teach language arts through a social justice lens. Included is the poem "Where I Am From" (p.18) where author George Ella Lyon describes her childhood with sensory detail. I like to share this poem with students because it invites them to recall their own lived experiences and, in writing about them, students' lives are brought to the classroom.

Before Writing

Begin a discussion with students on where everyone is from in the classroom. Begin with birthplaces. Next, ask students to describe their communities and neighbourhoods. What do they look like? Smell like? If a stranger strolled through their town, what would this person notice? Remember? Talk about back home? Ask students to choose one memory from growing up and narrow it down by recalling sensory details. Finally, read "Where I Am From." Ask students to turn to their neighbours and talk about one or two lines that stood out to them.

> I am from clothespins
> from chloride and carbon-tetrachloride
> I am from the dirt under the back porch
> (black, glistening, it tasted like beets)
> I am from the forsythia bush,
> The Dutch elm
> whose long gone limbs I remember
> as if they were my own.
>
> I am from fudge and eyeglasses,
> From Imogene and Alafair.
> I'm from the know-it-alls
> and the pass-it-ons,
> from perk up and pipe down.
> I'm from He restoreth my soul
> with a cottonball lamb
> and ten verses I can say myself.
>
> I'm from Artemus and Billie's Branch
> fried corn and strong coffee.
> from the finger my grandfather lost
> to the auger
> the eye my father shut to keep his sight.

CHAPTER 1

> Under my bed was a dress box
> spilling old pictures,
> a sift of lost faces
> to drift beneath my dreams.
> I am from those moments –
> snapped before I budded –
> leaf-fall from the family tree.

During Writing

Invite students to write their own narrative of Where I Am From. They may use a repeating pattern in the way Lyon does. Ask students to be specific in their writing, to push for particularity. Remind them that generalities in writing do not enliven treasured life moments.

After Writing

If students wrote their poems in stanzas, they may share one or more. While students are listening to each other share, ask them to write down the word or idea that resonates with them the most. How are they different and alike as other students in class? These kinds of connections can help students relate to one another, which is important work in building trust and a sense of community.

Sharing Student Writing

> I am from rosebushes and tomato plants
> from sunshine and photosynthesis
> I am from 900 square feet in suburban Detroit
> and the little Lutheran school
> whose playground lessons taught me so well.
>
> I am from be home before the street lights come on,
> the 8 tracks and vinyl,
> the shag carpet and model train sets,
> the corduroys, turtle necks, and polyester neckties.
> I'm from the piano lessons and hymns of praise,
> catechism classes and ancient creeds,
> Weekly Reader telling me that the wall just fell.
>
> I'm from the old country,
> Brandenburgs and Lammys,
> leaving Belfast and Pomerania behind.
> Dad was adopted when he was 2,

but I found out by accident when I was 17.
I thought I knew where he was from,
but now the mystery starts all over.
I am from right here, right now,
right where I started.
    -Bob

I am from a stubborn Opa, my Grandfather, and a perfect Grandma, my Oma;
I am from a family of two suitcases to the new country;
I am from a family who believed in new beginnings but lived some sad endings;
I am from a dedicated father who will always be my idol; and
I am from a caring mother.
    -Emmy

I am from cracks in the sidewalk and burned out streetlights.
I am from broken windows and a flickering porch light.
I am from sticky park benches and dried up popsicle.
I am from hardworking loving hands, from bills past due and notices on the door.
I am from the spot in the living room where the sun warmed the carpet, where the dog liked to sleep, where I rest my head, and closed my eyes.
I am from snug-as-a-bug-in-a-rug tuck-ins and good night prayers.
    -Martin

I am from nothing lasts forever.
I am from second chances, third one on the side.
I am from always pulling in two directions.
I am from consistently inconsistent and consistently consistent.
Still, I am from so much love and care.
I am from too many excuses and no excuses.
I am from hardly working and working hard.
I am from perfectly imperfect and too flawed.
I am from my own word.
I am from a rare place, from now on.
I am from my own destination.
    -Jordan

REFERENCE

Christensen, L. (2000). *Reading, writing, and rising up: Teaching about social justice and the power of the written word.* Milwaukee: WI: Rethinking Schools.

CHAPTER 1

MY REAL NAME IS

Susan Wooldridge's (1996) *Poemcrazy: Freeing Your Life with Words* is a collection of writing invitations designed to inspire and motivate people to write poetry. The poem, "My Real Name Is" (p. 38), invites students to think beyond their legal, given names or even nicknames. This writing prompt calls on students to consider invented or magical names they believe may better suit their personalities. I like to share this poem with students because it is identity building.

Before Writing

Begin a discussion with students on given names. In the discussion, include nicknames. Why do people give them to friends and family members? Also discuss fantasy names. For example, what name would they choose for themselves? Finally, read Ronnie's "My Real Name Is." Make a copy of the sentence starters so that students can see them on a white board, smart board, or overhead projector.

> Yesterday my name was James.
> Today it's tossing helium dream.
> Tomorrow my name will be
> Gerald Flying off the Cliff,
> Dave Mustang.
> Inside my heart is
> dying heart,
> sorrow
> guilt
> and a lotta hope.

> My real name is
> Yesterday my name was
> Today my name is
> Tomorrow my name will be
> My name once was
> In my dream my name was
> My _____ thinks my name is
> Secretly I know my name is

During Writing

Invite students to write their own My Real Name Is, completing all, most, or some of these sentence starters. If students do not want to write about themselves or want to write but feel uninspired by their names, they may put themselves into the role of something abstract (e.g., music) or someone else like a historical figure.

CORE STORIES

After Writing

Once students have finished writing, invite students to share what they have written. If students are sitting in groups, the teacher may invite one person from each group to share his/her writing. The teacher may also ask all students to read one line of their choosing or require that everyone read the same line (e.g., I secretly know my name is), creating a class poem of 'real names.'

Sharing Student Writing

> My real name is Dorthea Lange.
> Yesterday my name was questioned
> Today my name is controversy
> Tomorrow my name will be forgotten
> My name once was hero
> In my dream my name was remembered
> My friends think my name is important
> I secretly know my name lives on
>
>   -Windy

> My real name is music.
> Yesterday my name was noise.
> Today my name is hip hop.
> Tomorrow my name will be free to access.
> My name once was orchestral.
> In my dream my name was boundless.
> My audience thinks my name is life itself.
> Secretly, I know my name is subjective.
>
>   -John

> Yesterday my name was Unsure.
> Today my name is Social Anxiety.
>
> With the middle name Have Fun Anyway.
> Tomorrow my name will be Too Busy.
> In my dream my name was Freedom From All Labels.
> Secretly, I know my name is Hope.
>
>   -Carrie

My real name is Brent. Yesterday my name was In Question. Who? What? Where? Today my name is Confidence in something I know to be true filled with hope. Tomorrow my name will be Direction where I'll take my ship and plot a course, not where others tell me to go but where I feel I need to go. My name once was Insecure, Tossed Out, Unsure, Directionless. Really, I knew nothing of who I was or where I

CHAPTER 1

wanted to go. In my dream, my name was Possible where anything could happen. I could go anywhere and be anything. My critics think my name is Limited. Secretly, I know my name is Anything I choose to be.
    -Brent

My name is Rob Gordon, hopeless romantic and eternally looking at what was. Tomorrow my name will be Dumbfounded, realizing the gravity and soul of what today really is, one day too late.
    -Mike

REFERENCE

Wooldridge, S. (1996) *Poemcrazy: Freeing your life with words.* New York, NY: Three Rivers Press.

SIX-WORD MEMOIR

Editors Rachel Fershleiser and Larry Smith's (2008) *Not Quite What I Was Planning: Six-Word Memoirs by Writers Famous & Obscure* includes a collection of true tales from well-known authors to ordinary people from around the world. These memoirs, captured in just six words, range from the serious to the hilarious, each one an example of someone's lived experience. I like to share six-word memoirs with students because it requires them to think carefully about word choice and allows them to experience the power of certain words, whether they entertain or capture a moment in time. Writing six-word memoirs also teaches students about brevity by learning to omit unnecessary words.

Before Writing

Begin a discussion with students on important events in their lives. What are they? Which events were the most defining? Ask students to reflect on one or two events that stand out the most. Next, read a selection of six-word memoirs from the book.

    Afraid of everything. Did it anyway. Ayse Erginer (p.42)
    Four children in four decades; whew! Loeretta Serrano (p. 53)
    Meat and potatoes man goes vegetarian. Parette Lawrence (p. 67)
    Never really finished anything, except cake. Carletta Perkins (p. 85)
    I write because I can't sleep. Ben Mezrich (p. 110)
    Detergent girl: Bold. Tide. Cheer. All. Martha Clarkson (p. 180)
    Five continents down; two to go. Virginia Graham (p. 183)
    Afraid of mirrors, too many marshmallows. Lihi Lasslo (p. 196)
    Wasn't born a redhead; fixed that. Andie Grace (p. 218)
    Loved home. Left to make sue. Adam Krefman (p. 220)

During Writing

Invite students to write their own Six-Word Memoir. Students may write about a specific event in their lives or address broader themes like lessons learned. Encourage students to write more than one memoir.

After Writing

Students may share their memoirs in small groups. Invite one person from each group to read a memoir, giving the class an opportunity to guess who the memoir is about.

CHAPTER 1

Sharing Student Writing

> Clutter: A burden that never lightens.
> Swimming in a sea of ephemera.
> Clothing bondage thy name is sale.
> The family circus comes to town.
> My bike collects cobwebs not miles.
>
> -Sheila

> Alone with people all around me.
>
> -Laura

> I stood up while sitting down.
>
> -Tierra, on *Rosa Parks*

> Love you always. May not like.
>
> -Lauren

REFERENCE

Fershleiser, R., & Smith, L. (2008). *Not quite what I was planning: Six-word memoirs by writers famous & obscure.* New York, NY: HarperCollins.

IF YOU REALLY KNEW ME

Challenge Day (www.challengeday.org) is a national movement in Canada and the United States that honours and celebrates diversity, truth, and self-expression. Standing in a circle, a line, or small groups (also called a line-around), students one-by-one complete the sentence starter, "If You Really Knew Me" as a powerful vehicle to express aspects about themselves that are unknown to others. I watched high school students try this engagement on the Oprah Winfrey Show and second grade teacher Regi Matheny and I tried it with second graders in my dissertation study. I like to use this engagement with students because it provides opportunities to be bold in writing by identifying what they hide about themselves from others.

Before Writing

Begin a discussion with students on what it means to know someone. What kinds of things do they notice about a person? (e.g., teams they play on, organizations they belong to, church they attend). What kinds of things do they generally not know about a person? (e.g., a divorced parent, a disability, a boy/girlfriend in secret, struggles with gender identity, etc.). Next, ask students to mentally finish the sentence, "If you really knew me you would know..." Finally, read Kamryn's response to the prompt.

"If you really knew me you would know that I'm biracial. My mom is white and my dad is black. If you really knew me you would know that I love Clemson and my nickname is FROG because every time my parents hug me close, I stick to them like a frog."

During Writing

Invite students to write their own If You Really Knew Me, a few statements that capture their core personality. Encourage students to take some risks in their writing by addressing aspects about themselves they want others to know.

After Writing

In a line-around, invite students to share one *If You Really Knew Me* statement until everyone in the room has had an opportunity to share. For students unsure of sharing, they can say, "Pass" until the next person shares.

Sharing Student Writing

> If you really knew me you would know that I lost a cousin to Cystic Fibrosis.
> I've lost both parents at an early age.
> My parents and little sister are moving to Colorado in February.

CHAPTER 1

I started to write a novel in grade eight.
I have a rock collection.
I'm an avid blood donor.
I used to weigh 300lbs.
I'm a quiet person.

  -Anonymous

If you really knew me you know that I can be really bossy.
That I didn't know anything about fashion until my mid 20's.
That I use my height to seem braver than I am.
That I'd smoke if it wasn't unhealthy.
I'd like to get in one good physical fight.

  -Megan

If you really knew me you would know I hate wearing makeup.
If you really knew me you would know I don't eat as well as I should.
If you really knew me you would know I lost a good friend when I was seventeen.
If you really knew me you would know I'm quite ignorant when it comes to politics.
If you really knew me you would know I read my favourite books over and over.
If you really knew me you would know I am sceptical about religion.
If you really knew me you would know my brother is the most important person in my life.
If you really knew me you would know I have a terrible memory.

  -Briana

REFERENCE

www.challengeday.org

WHEN YOU LEFT

I collect magazine and newspaper ads because they often provide inspiration for writing. "When You Left" is an investment ad from Price Water House Coopers. Through a series of questions aimed at looking at the whole person, the ad emphasizes the importance of being true to oneself. I like to share this ad with students because it invites them to examine what aspects of their lives are true and yet easily forgotten in the day to day.

Before Writing

Begin a discussion with students on rushing out the door. What kinds of things do they usually forget? (e.g., car keys, packed lunch, homework, gym shoes). Next, direct the conversation to themselves; what corners of their lives do they leave behind whenever they leave home to go somewhere? What part of themselves do they forget about, keep tucked away and private? Finally, read the following investment ad.

> When you left for work this morning, what did you leave behind?
> Your opinions?
> Your background?
> Your earring?
> Your native tongue?
> Your doubts?
> Your children?
> Your secrets?
> Your real hairstyle?
> Your race?
> Your politics?
> Your ethnicity?
> Your gender?
> Your sexual orientation?
> Your personality?
> Your uniqueness?
> Your ideas?
> Yourself?

A workplace can only be diverse if the people who work there can be themselves.

During Writing

Ask the question, "When you left for *class* this morning, what did you leave behind?" and invite students to write a few sentences of their own When You Left. Though students cannot use examples from the ad (e.g., my politics), they may draw inspiration from it by being specific (e.g., my views on healthcare).

CHAPTER 1

After Writing

Invite students to read one line from their notebooks until everyone in the room has had an opportunity to share. For students unsure of sharing, they can say, "Pass." Close the writing engagement with the statement, "A *classroom* can only be diverse if the people who *learn* there can be themselves."

Sharing Student Writing

>My lunch
>My burdens
>My key to work
>My messy bedroom and bathroom
>My boyfriend of 8 years
>I forgot to tell my dad to be safe at work. He is a police officer.
>
>>-Anonymous

When I left for work this morning, I left behind the tired student I am. I became, instead, a working adult that forgets her personal life.
>>-Jessica

>When I left your eager face,
>You were hoping I'd bring you with me.
>Your smile, showing your bottom teeth,
>turned suddenly disheartened
>as
>I
>shut
>the
>door
>and you raced to the window.
>
>>-Whitney

REFERENCE

www.pwc.com

CORE STORIES

FOOD MEMOIR

Nigel Slater's (2003) *Toast: The Story of a Boy's Hunger* is a memoir about his childhood in England. What stands out to me in Slater's writing is his ability to describe food in such vivid and creative detail. I like to share Slater's food memoirs with students because by reflecting on their own food histories, students are called to describe not just the foods they loved and loathed but perhaps more importantly the associations that exist between the people in their lives and their food memories (Gallagher, 2011). Greta Vollmer, professor of English at Sonoma State University, calls this engagement *What My Childhood Tasted Like.*

Before Writing

Begin a discussion with students on food memories from childhood. Start with reading the lines "It is impossible not to love someone who makes toast for you" (p.1) and "Cake holds a family together" (p. 4). Ask students which foods hold their family together and talk about the foods they enjoy, especially when made for them by someone they love. Finally, read the three excerpts below from *Toast*. They emphasize a much-loved food, a much-hated food, and a food that has rules.

> I love bread-and-butter pudding. I love its layers of sweet, quivering custard, juicy raisins, and puffed, golden crust. I love the way it sings quietly in the oven; the way it wobbles on the spoon. You can't smell a hug. You can't hear a cuddle. But if you could, I reckon it would smell and sound of warm bread-and-butter pudding (p. 7).

> Without a word he stabs his fork into a slice of ham and slaps it on my plate. A hot wave of hate goes through my body. Hate ham, hate him. Actually, I rather like ham. What I don't like is this ham. The sort of ham that comes from an oval green tin and is surrounded by golden-brown jelly. The sort of ham it takes an age to pry from its aluminium coffin. The sort of ham my father carves very thinly with the same knife he uses for the Sunday roast. Pretty pink ham, evil jelly (p. 31).

> The turkey stew...varied from year to year, but the trifle had rules. He used ready-made Swiss rolls...They had to be filled with raspberry jam, never apricot because you couldn't see the swirl of jam through the glass bowl the way you could with raspberry. There was much giggling over the sherry bottle...Next, a tin of peaches with a little of their syrup. He was meticulous about soaking the sponge roll. First the sherry, then the syrup from the peaches tin. Then the jelly. To the purists the idea of jelly in trifle is anathema. But to my father it was essential...He would make bright yellow custard, Bird's from a tin. This he smothered over the jelly, taking an almost absurd amount of care

CHAPTER 1

not to let the custard run between the Swiss roll slices and the glass. A matter of honour, no doubt. Once it was cold, the custard was covered with whipped cream, glacé cherries, and whole blanched almonds. Never silver balls, which he thought common, or chocolate vermicelli, which he thought made it sickly. Just big fat almonds. He never toasted them, even though it would have made them taste better. In later years my step-mother was to suggest a sprinkling of multi-coloured hundreds and thousands. She might as well have suggested changing his daily paper to the *Mirror* (p. 9).

During Writing

Invite students to write their own Food Memoir, a narrative that illuminates one food memory from their childhood. They can write about a much-loved food, a much-hated food, or a food that had rules growing up.

After Writing

Given that these written narratives will be longer, invite two or three students to share their food memoirs. If there is little time to share, the teacher may invite students to do a line-around where students take turns and volunteer to read a line from their narratives.

Sharing Student Writing

> Red meat. I love the flavour of beef stewed with vegetables, onions, potatoes, and baby carrots. But the meat fools me every time. I stir the stew pot and can always find a white, gelatinous glob of fat. It usually giggles on a piece of beef. It laughs at me. I wrinkle my nose and place it back in the pot, helping myself to more potatoes and carrots. I get a glass of water. When I return, someone has heaped more stew into my bowl and I can see fat, white and glistening. I feel sick. I take a knife and remove the fat with surgical precision. Smiling, I take a bite and then I feel it; an unmistakable squishy gummy substance on my tongue. I missed a bit.
>   -Nate

> I hate plain white bread. Frankly, I don't understand why anyone would waste time and money on plain white bread. It has no real flavour, texture, or character. White bread is like sex without commitment, connection, or enjoyment.
>   -Sheila

> It is impossible not to love someone who makes dolma for you. Someone who picks grape leaves, boils them, and then wraps them with a homemade family recipe of meat, rice, and spices – just for you. Words cannot explain the joy

I feel when my mom tells me she's making it for dinner. There are no words to describe the happiness on my tongue when I savour a cooked leaf. Even though I just had it for dinner last night, the cartwheel in my belly tells me I want more.

-Raghad

Chop Suey. It really should be called worms; slimy, cold, and disgusting. Cold, because I just sit there. Sit. Sit. Waiting. Waiting for I don't know what. It really should just be called chop ew-y.

-Whitney

When I think about chicken noodle soup, I think about cold winter days and my grandpa. This is the soup my Grandpa would make me every time I was sick. This is the soup my Grandpa would bring to my house and make sure it was warm at lunchtime. This is the soup my Grandpa would always make sure I had extra on my birthday. Whenever I have chicken noodle, I remember the love my Grandpa had for me.

-Jean

REFERENCES

Gallagher, K. (2011). *Write like this: Teaching real-world writing through modelling & mentor texts.* Portland, ME: Stenhouse.

Slater, N. (2003). *Toast: The story of a boy's hunger.* New York, NY: Gotham.

CHAPTER 1

BECAUSE I AM

Because I Am a Girl (www.becauseiamagirl.ca) is a social movement toward investing in girls and women in dire areas and situations at home and in the developing world as key to eliminating poverty. The initiative also impacts boys and men as gender equality cannot be addressed by one gender alone. I like to share this ad with students because it asks them to reflect on what it means to be who they are (or who they feel they are becoming) as well as what their gender could mean if they lived somewhere else in the world.

Before Writing

Begin a discussion with students on gender equality. What kind of advantages and disadvantages are there to being a girl? A boy? Next, ask students to consider what advantages/disadvantages exist for other roles such as being a sibling, a cousin, an aunt, an uncle, a parent, a grandparent, a wife, a husband, a boy/girlfriend? Finally, read "Because I am a Girl."

> Because I am a girl, I watch my brothers go to school while I stay home.
> Because I am a girl, I eat if there's food left over when everyone is done.
> Because I am a girl, I am the poorest of the poor.
> Because I am a girl, I will share what I know.
> Because I am a girl, I am the heart of my community.
> Because I am a girl, I will pull my family out of poverty if you give me the chance.
> Because I am a girl, I will take what you invest in me and uplift everyone around me.
> Because I am a girl, I can change the world.

During Writing

Invite students to write their own Because I Am statements. Students may choose to be gender specific (e.g., Because I am a girl; Because I am a boy) or select a role instead (e.g., Because I am a sister, a boyfriend, a hockey player, etc.).

After Writing

Invite individual students to share at random what they have written. The teacher may also group students by their subject (e.g., Let us hear from those who wrote about being a girl. Next, let us hear from those who wrote about being a boy).

Sharing Student Writing

> Because I am 11, I can't drive
> Because I am 11, I don't have a credit card

Because I am 11, I can't buy an airsoft gun online without my mom putting her information in
Because I am 11, I can't play basketball on my school team
Because I am 11, I can't play travel basketball
Because I am 11, I can't even get a job
Because I am 11, I can't see a movie at the movie theatre by myself
Because I am 11, I don't have an I.D.
But because I am 11, I can stay up late when my friends come over.

    -Alex, Grade 6

Because I am different, I don't like to be all fancy. No dresses. No skirts. No tights!
Because I am different, I like catching frogs and salamanders and playing with them, too. Who cares if I get slimy and gooey?
Because I am different, I'm ok with getting dirty especially in science. Some girls say "eeewww" but I say "awesome."
Because I am different, I am me.

    -Ashley, Grade 6

Because I am in an interracial relationship, I am sometimes considered a whore.
Because I am in an interracial relationship, I must like to get hurt.
Because I am in an interracial relationship, my boyfriend will one day cheat on me.
Because I am in an interracial relationship, I got ousted from my family.
Because I am in an interracial relationship, I must be "stealing all their good men."
But because I am in an interracial relationship, I see all people through accepting eyes.

    -Valerie

Because I am single I have no one to call when I'm having a rough day.
Because I am single I have no one to take me out to dinner or the movies.
Because I am single I have no one to cuddle up with and keep me warm at night.
Because I am single I have no one to share my hopes and dreams with.
Because I am single I have no one to tell, "I love you."
But, because I am single, I can do whatever the hell I want and share those experiences with anyone and everyone I please. I am happy being alone and just being me.

    -Heather

REFERENCE

www.becauseiamagirl.ca

CHAPTER 1

EVERYBODY NEEDS

Byrd Baylor's (1974) *Everybody Needs a Rock* is a picture book about a boy who offers 10 rules on how to find the perfect rock. Inspired by the structure of this text, fifth-grade student Stephanie Miller wrote, "Everybody Needs a Father" (p. 116) as cited in Fletcher's (1996) *A Writer's Notebook: Unlocking the Writer Within You*. I like to share Miller's narrative with students because in a social climate where wants and needs are often confused, this engagement asks students to think about what is essential in their lives.

Before Writing

Begin a discussion with students on collecting objects. What are some common (e.g., rocks, seashells, marbles, sports cards, and stamps) and uncommon collectible items? What significance do these objects hold for them? Next, read "Everybody Needs a Father" and discuss the repeating pattern in this piece of writing.

> Everybody needs
> a father.
> Fatherless
> children are always
> trying to fight
> their fears away.
> You can't just
> pick any father,
> he has to be a
> special one just
> for you. I know
> this girl in
> Arizona that
> picked the wrong
> father and
> ended up
> running away
> and never came
> back. If you
> don't know who to
> pick lemme tell
> you some rules
> to getting just
> the right father.
>
> #1 It doesn't
> matter what your

CORE STORIES

father looks like.
You gotta see
way into his soul
to pick the right
one. I know this
boy in Texas
who picked a
father because
he was handsome,
and his father
left him. Just left
without even saying
good-bye.

#2 You gotta pick
somebody who'll
spend time
with you.
Somebody who'll
go for walks
in the woods
with you and
take you on
trips. Trips that
take you
halfway across
California
but only
seem
like ten minutes 'cause
you're having such
a good time.

#3 Pick a father
who likes the sound
of little feet
around the
house and
doesn't mind
a fight with
your brother
once in a while.

CHAPTER 1

During Writing

Invite students to write their own narrative of Everybody Needs. Students may write about an object they genuinely collect or something more abstract in the way Stephanie Mille talks about needing a dad. Students may also prefer to write their narrative in free verse. Like Baylor and Miller, their narrative should include some rules.

After Writing

Invite two or three students to share their narratives or free verse poems. If there is little time to share, the teacher may start a line-around where students take turns and volunteer to read their first line (e.g., everybody needs a _____) and/or one of their rules.

Sharing Student Writing

Everybody needs a green space.
Leafy and shadowy to cool the hot hiss of anger and grief.
Flat and smooth to cradle one's body into forgiveness and surrender.
Rolling and mountainous to rest one's weary soul and eyes for just a few minutes once a day, once a month, once a year.
          -Sheila

Everybody needs a home.
Don't pick a home that's someone else's.
Make sure your home is your own.
Make sure it's not too quiet.
Your home may not be what you expected.
It may not be your choice.
But fill it with love.
Always pick a home with a dog in mind.
Because everyone needs a dog.
A dog will love you.
A dog will always be your home.
Everybody needs a home.
          -Whitney

Everyone needs a bathing suit. Without one, how would you cool off in the summer?
#1 Pick a bathing suit that's the right colour. You want the colour of your bathing suit to express the kind of person you are.

#2 Pick a bathing suit that makes you feel comfortable. You want one that you can swim in, lay out in, and run around in.

#3 Pick a bathing suit that no one else has. I once went to the beach and someone was wearing the same suit as me. Did she look better?

#4 Pick a bathing suit that doesn't leave you with a weird tan line. That is the worst.

    -Kristen

Everybody needs hope.

#1. If you don't have hope it is most likely you will die inside. You need hope when you're surrounded by lions. Trust me. Once a person didn't have hope when he was surrounded by lions and a person saved him.

#2. Hope also helps you stay calm in an emergency. For example, if there was a twister outside and you didn't have hope you'd be screaming. But if you did have hope you'd be scared but not screaming.

#3. You even need hope in the weirdest problems, like if a gorilla who wants to rip your face off was chasing you. In that situation you'd need hope.

#4. If you have hope good things will happen to you. When you have hope in a problem that problem will go away. Hope helps you live more smoothly.

    -Brody, Grade 2

REFERENCES

Baylor, B. (1974). *Everybody needs a rock.* New York, NY: Alladin.

Fletcher, R. (1996). *A writer's notebook: Unlocking the writer within you.* New York, NY: HarperCollins.

CHAPTER 1

THE OUTSIDE ME, THE INSIDE ME

Meredith Sue Willis' (2000) *Personal Fiction Writing: A Guide to Writing from Real Life for Teachers, Students & Writers* includes over 400 writing assignments. I came across one of those assignments in Sam Swope's (2005) *I Am a Pencil: A Teacher, His Kids, and Their World of Stories,* a three-year writer's workshop study with 28 students in grades three, four, and five. Third grade writer Su Jung's "The Outside Me, The Inside Me" (p. 53) describes how she sees herself. The outside me describes the way one looks to others (e.g., physical descriptions, behaviour, personality); the inside me describes what nobody sees. I like to share Su Jung's short narrative with students because her writing speaks honestly and reflectively about how she sees herself and provides a model for how students can write their own personal reflection. From http://www.languageisavirus.com, American poet Bernadette Mayer takes a similar approach, inviting writers to write what is personally secret and what is shared and experiment with both veiled and direct language. From *Trust the Process: An Artist's Guide to Letting Go,* author Shaun McNiff (1998) recommends looking at the self in terms of illumination and shadow, asking the questions, "What stands in the light? In the darkness?" (p. 103). Sometimes, I use these questions to help guide discussions with students about the inside/outside me, reminding them that what stands in shadow or darkness does not have to be negative but rather deep and powerful.

Before Writing

Begin a discussion with students on perception. How do they see themselves? How do they perceive others and how do others perceive them? What milestones or achievement have they achieved that no one knows about? What secrets do they keep? What do they hide about themselves from others? Finally, read Su Jung's "The Outside Me, The Inside Me."

> *The Outside Me*
> I have black hair and brown eyes. I always tie my hair before I come to school. I wear jeans almost every day. My skin colour is peach. I am tall. I have short hair. I wear sneakers most of the time.
> *The Inside me*
> I am unhappy all the time.

Explain to students that *The Inside Me* section does not have to be serious. Some of Jung's peers took a more light-hearted approach to writing about themselves that nobody sees. Aaron wrote, "The me nobody sees is my Batman underwear' (p. 54). Others were more whimsical (e.g., Nicole: "Inside I am the wind of peace") or literal (e.g., Cesar: "Inside me I have a brain, a heart, stomach, guts, and blood"). In sum, there is more than one way to approach this writing engagement.

CORE STORIES

During Writing

Invite students to write their own narrative of The Outside Me, The Inside Me. Students are encouraged, though not required, to write anything private in the *Inside Me* section because their audience for the notebook is always themselves.

After Writing

Students may share one or two lines from their narratives from either both sections or just one.

Sharing Student Writing

> The Outside Me: I have hazel eyes and my hair is multi-coloured and long. I am short and skinny. People say I have chicken legs. My hair may be a mess but my nails are always perfectly done. I usually dress comfortably and wear flip flops. I'm very friendly and often smiling.
> The Inside Me: I am very insecure.
>
> -Andrea

> The outside me has roots of blonde showing through fake brown hair, green eyes, a small smile, and comfortable clothes specifically picked out to make me feel skinny because the inside me has body image issues and always has.
>
> -Valerie

> On the outside:
> I am blonde;
> I have hazel eyes;
> I am healthy;
> I am outgoing;
> I am arrogant;
> I am talkative;
> I am a bad-ass;
> I am friendly;
> I achieve a lot and rarely fail; and
> I am worry free.
> But really on the inside I am very shy and often lack confidence.
>
> -Brian

> The outside me is extremely tall; my friends call me Heather long legs. I have hazel eyes and auburn hair. A bit burlesque, some might say. The inside me is proud of my humour, friendliness, and personality but quite ashamed of my personal body image.
>
> -Heather

25

CHAPTER 1

REFERENCES

http://www.languageisavirus.com

McNiff, S. (1998). *Trust the process: An artist's guide to letting go.* Boston, MA: Shambhala.

Swope, S. (2005). *I am a pencil: A teacher, his kids, and their world of stories.* New York, NY: Henry Holt.

Willis, M. S. (2000). *Personal fiction writing: A guide to writing from real life for teachers, students & writers.* New York, NY: Teachers and Writers Collaborative.

FAMILY TREASURE

The features article "What's your favourite family treasure?" comes from the March 2011 issue of the Canadian magazine *Chatelaine*. Included are six short narratives from people across Canada who remember an object (e.g., a pair of gold cufflinks, silverware, recorded tapes, wooden serving tray) that they inherited and/or have enjoyed over the years. I like to share these stories with students because they speak to the human experience of collecting and cherishing things that matter. The writing honours and preserves the memory of those who have given us objects we hold dear.

Before Writing

Begin a discussion with students on personal items that matter to them. Do they have any objects that were passed down to them? Is there a family treasure they hope will be passed down to them one day? A family treasure can also be a favourite dish or family ritual (e.g., going someplace each year). Next, read two selected stories from "What's your favourite family treasure?"

> My mother's red dancing shoes. I can still see my mom and dad gliding smoothly around the floor – a lovely, romantic memory for a daughter to have of her parents. Many years ago, after dad passed away, Mom brought out her shoes for me to try on, and they fit perfectly! I will pass those dancing shoes on to my daughter and then my granddaughter. I've worn them to family functions many times. Mom, at 91, gets a charge out of seeing her shoes again, and likes to try them on "just for fun."
>
>   -Kathy Dale, Guelph, Ontario

> My late husband was born in an outport village on the coast of Newfoundland. Homes at the time didn't have running water, so a pitcher and basin set were used. I have a photo of my husband being bathed in a set in 1939, and another photo of our eldest son, David, being bathed in the same basin in 1967 on his first visit to Grand Bruit, as running water still hadn't arrived. The set came to me in the '70s, and the memories of my "older and gentler time" come back in a flash whenever I look at it.
>
>   -Joan Ingram, Margaree, Nova Scotia

During Writing

Invite students to write about their own Family Treasure or one they hope to have one day, such as inheriting an object by a certain age. Ask students to include some sensory details (e.g., touch, smell, taste, see, and hear) when describing their family treasure. This kind of attention to language (e.g., the *click*-sound my grandfather's pocket watch made when I closed it) can help bring the memory to life.

CHAPTER 1

After Writing

The teacher may organize student sharing by those who wrote about treasures they have and treasures they hope to have one day.

Sharing Student Writing

> Sunday lunch at Aunt Dorothy's. Mom always said that her sister was the kind of woman who'd "go clear across town to save twenty-five cents on a can of green beans." Her penny-pinching ways always produced my favourite: crispy fried chicken judiciously seasoned with salt and pepper that crackled with each mouthful and bargain green beans flavoured with thickly sliced pink ham hocks. Buttered corn bread wafted through the small kitchen. Sweet potatoes clothed in their Georgia clay coloured jackets sparkled with butter, sugar, and cinnamon. I gladly and thankfully washed this all down with my aunt's darkly brewed sweet tea with lemon that made my ears ring and sent shivers down my back.
>
>   -Sheila

> A little weathered and rusty now, but you can still see the red, yellow, blue, white, green license plates. From 1962-1978 my father nailed the license plates from our first family cars to the rafters of our garage ceiling. While spinning on a swing or dangling upside down on the jungle gym, I would see them and try to remember which car was attached to each plate. The years with just one license plate meant that my dad took the train to and from work if my mom needed the car. It continues to be a fond memory of seeing my dad wave to us while he stood on the steps of the train as it pulled into the station. When my mother is gone, I hope to remove a few of the plates and hang them in my garage.
>
>   -Susan

REFERENCE

What's your favourite family treasure? (2011, March). *Chatelaine*, 22.

FORGIVENESS POEM

Linda Christensen's (2000) *Reading, Writing, and Rising Up: Teaching about Social Justice and the Power of the Written Word* provides a collection of ideas on how to teach language arts through a social justice lens. Included is the poem, "Forgiving My Mother" (p. 67) by student writer Tanya Park. I like to share this poem with students because forgiveness involves a range of emotions - anger, disappointment, guilt, and regret. Park's simple yet powerful double repeating pattern (e.g., For all the times; I forgive you) offers students a model with which they can grapple their own range of emotions about forgiving someone or something. Other good poems worth reading to deepen the conversation on writing about forgiveness include Clifton's (1989) *Forgiving My Father* and Robert P. Tristram Coffin's (1949) *Forgive My Guilt*.

Before Writing

Begin a discussion with students on forgiveness. What does it mean to truly forgive someone? Who do they forgive? Who do they struggle to forgive and why? What makes forgiveness difficult for some, easy for others? Next, read "Forgiving My Mother."

> For all the times you yelled
> and all the times you screamed
> I forgive you.
>
> For all the nights we had breakfast
> for dinner and dinner for breakfast
> I forgive you.
>
> For all the times I felt you pushed
> my daddy away
> I forgive you.
>
> For all the times we ran away
> and came back,
> For all the times we packed
> and unpacked,
>
> for all the friends I've lost
> and all the schools I've seen,
>
> for all the times
> I was the new kid on the scene,
> I forgive you.

CHAPTER 1

During Writing

Invite students to write their own Forgiveness Poem. Encourage students to create a pattern in their writing. Like Park, students may want to use stanzas and repetition of a particular phrase (e.g., "For all the…").

After Writing

Invite a few students to share their poems. If using stanzas, some students may prefer to only share one or two and keeping the rest private.

Sharing Student Writing

> For being shy until I was in my forties
> For wanting someone else's hair and body
> I forgive myself.
> For listening to every voice, but my own
> For caring much too much about appearances or being liked
> I forgive myself.
> For not being the main course in my own life
> For making a man, a job, or a friendship
> the appetizer, entrée, and dessert of my life
> year after year
> I forgive myself.
> For being a slow learner
> I forgive myself.
>
>   -Sheila

For all the times you forgot to go outside,
I forgive you.
For barking all night until you got to sleep in my bed,
I forgive you.
For all the times you barked as if ready to kill,
I forgive you.
For all the times you brought me an unwanted gift from outside,
I forgive you.
For qualifying for private $200 obedience classes,
I forgive you.

      -Liz

For all the times
you mistreated my mom
I forgive you

For all the times
you were not there to help
I forgive you

For all the times
you broke your promises
I forgive you.

For all the times
I did not understand why you did what you did
I forgive you
        -Tina

REFERENCES

Christensen, L. (2000). *Reading, writing, and rising up: Teaching about social justice and the power of the written word.* Milwaukee: WI: Rethinking Schools.
Clifton, L. (1989). *Good woman: Poems and memoir 1969–1980.* Rochester, NY: BOA Editions.
Coffin, R. P. T. (1949). Forgive my guilt. *Atlantic Monthly,* 60.

CHAPTER 1

PRAISE POEM

Linda Christensen's (2000) *Reading, Writing, and Rising Up: Teaching about Social Justice and the Power of the Written Word* provides a collection of ideas on how to teach language arts through a social justice lens. Included is the poem, "What the Mirror Said" (p. 53) by student writer Curtina Barr. I like to share this poem with students because self-praise is not easy, particularly for adolescents and young adults; however, Barr picks a familiar lens (i.e. mirror) for self-examination that students can relate to and invites them to write something praiseful about themselves.

Before Writing

Begin a discussion with students on praise. What is praise? What does it mean to praise something or someone? How do they show praise to others, to their culture, to their heritage? Next, read "What the Mirror Said."

> The mirror told me,
> "Yo' skin the colour of coffee
> after the cream's been poured in.
> Yo' body's just the right size –
> not too plump,
> not too thin.
> Yo' lips like cotton candy
> sweet and soft.
> Yo' sho' done good.
> Yo' like a city,
> strong and tall,
> though deep in yo' eyes
> I can still see yo' pain,
> yo' smile and laugh.
> Keep doin' yo' thang.

During Writing

Invite students to write their own Praise Poem. Some students may prefer to write an Ode to something or someone.

After Writing

Invite two or three students to share their praise poem.

Sharing Student Writing

The mirror told me,
Your skin's the colour of melted toffee
straight out of a candy shop.
Your face glitters with beauty spots
like monuments that dot beautiful cities.
Your eyes are bay windows
that say hard work and dedication.
Your shoulders are strained and toned,
a stallion after a good run.
Your smile is smothered in sweetness
and sometimes lies, like a child to her mother.
You are accepting and welcome new challenges.
Your feet tread endless possibilities.
    -Nicole

~The mirror told me I was blessed with good looks~
a dashing Neil Patrick Harris and a wonder for the books.
~Whether it's my amazing eyes or my chiseled chest~
my character sure sets me apart from the rest.
~So gaze on me with amazement and please your eyes~
Yes, you got it! A shake comes with these fries.
    -Brian

REFERENCE

Christensen, L. (2000). *Reading, writing, and rising up: Teaching about social justice and the power of the written word.* Milwaukee: WI: Rethinking Schools.

CHAPTER 1

TWO-VOICE POEM

Paul Fleischman's (1988) *Joyful Noise: Poems for Two Voices* illuminates perspective beautifully through a collection of fourteen two-voice poems about insects. Included is the poem "Honeybees" (p. 29) where the queen and worker bee's voices are distinctive and clear. Reading two-voice poems requires two readers or two groups of readers where one side reads the left-hand part and the other reads the right-hand part. Text on the same line is read simultaneously. I like to share this poem with students because it can be challenging writing another perspective on a topic or issue. This poem invites students to look inside themselves to find their own perspective on something before writing the other side. Tell students that three and four-voice poems also exist such as Fleischman's (2008) *Big Talk: Poems for Four Voices*. For students more interested in math than science, Pappas' (1993) *Math Talk: Mathematical Ideas in Poems for Two Voices* is worth a second look.

Before Writing

Begin a discussion with students on voice. In particular, ask students to discuss contrasting voices (e.g., mother/daughter; father/son; coach/player; boyfriend/girlfriend). Which voices dominate? What kinds of words are characteristic of particular roles? Ask students to think about what their voice sounds like in some of their own relationships. Next, read "Honeybees."

Being a bee	Being a bee
	is a joy.
is a pain.	
	I'm a queen
I'm a worker	
I'll gladly explain.	I'll gladly explain.
	Upon rising, I'm fed
	By my royal attendants,
I'm up at dawn, guarding	
the hive's narrow entrance	
	I'm bathed
then I take out	
the hive's morning trash	
	then I'm groomed.
Then I put in an hour	
making wax,	
without two minutes' time	
to sit still and relax.	
	The rest of my day
	is quite simply set forth:

then I might collect nectar from the field three miles north	
	I lay eggs,
or perhaps I'm on larva detail	
	by the hundred.
feeding the grubs in their cells, wishing that *I* were still helpless and pale:	
	I'm loved and I'm lauded, I'm outranked by none.
Then I pack combs with Pollen – not my idea of fun.	
	When I've done enough laying
Then, weary, I strive	
	I retire
to patch up any cracks in the hive.	
	for the rest of the day.
Then I build some new cells, slaving away at enlarging this Hell, dreading the sight of another sunrise, wondering why we don't all unionize.	
Truly, a bee's is the worst	Truly, a bee's is the best
of all lives.	of all lives.

During Writing

Invite students to write their own Two-Voice Poem. Remind students that each voice should be distinctive. Encourage students to write a two-voice poem about one of their own relationships or someone else's relationship (e.g., a girl writing about the way her boyfriend and dad talk to each other).

CHAPTER 1

After Writing

The teacher may pair students to read two-voice poems. The writer should feel comfortable sharing his/her writing with the partner.

Sharing Student Writing

Get Moving!	
	Why do I have to leave my home?
You don't pay your rent; Go!	
	How expensive this world has become.
Complain! Complain!	
	Expenses, expenses.
I'll show them.	
	We're ruined.
Why buy something you can't afford?	
	I didn't plan to lose my job.
Why not plan ahead?	
	I didn't plan for my child to become ill.
Excuses, Excuses.	
	I'm trying, I'm trying.
Must be lazy.	
	I've taken two jobs.
	(deep sigh)
Debt!	Debt.
	-Kristen

REFERENCES

Fleischman, P. (1988). *Joyful noise: Poems for two voices.* New York, NY: HarperCollins.
Fleischman, P. (2008). *Big talk: Poems for four voices.* Somerville, MA: Candlewick.
Pappas, T. (1993). *Math talk: Mathematical ideas in poems for two voices.* San Carlos, CA: Wide World Publishing.

MY NAME

Sandra Cisneros' (1984) *The House on Mango Street* is a heart-warming and heartbreaking story told in a series of vignettes about a Latina girl, Esperanza Cordero, growing up in Chicago. In "My Name" (p.10), Esperanza details several aspects about her name, a lot of which she does not like. "To say the name," according to Swampy Cree Indians, "is to begin the story" (Christensen, 2000, p.10). I like sharing this vignette with students because it calls on them to begin their story by writing what they know about their name. The writing engagement may also reveal how students feel about themselves, as influenced by their name.

Before Writing

Begin a discussion with students on what they know about their given names. Do they know what they mean? Are they named after a family member, a movie star, or a character in a book? Do they identify more with their middle name? What thoughts and feelings do they have about their surnames? Next, read "My Name."

> In English my name means hope. In Spanish it means too many letters. It means sadness, it means waiting. It is like the number nine. A muddy colour. It is the Mexican records my father plays on Sunday mornings when he is shaving, songs like sobbing.
>
> It was my great-grandmother's name and now it is mine. She was a horse woman too, born like me in the Chinese year of the horse--which is supposed to be bad luck if you're born female-but I think this is a Chinese lie because the Chinese, like the Mexicans, don't like their women strong.
>
> My great-grandmother. I would've liked to have known her, a wild, horse of a woman, so wild she wouldn't marry. Until my great-grandfather threw a sack over her head and carried her off. Just like that, as if she were a fancy chandelier. That's the way he did it.
>
> And the story goes she never forgave him. She looked out the window her whole life, the way so many women sit their sadness on an elbow. I wonder if she made the best with what she got or was she sorry because she couldn't be all the things she wanted to be. Esperanza. I have inherited her name, but I don't want to inherit her place by the window.
>
> At school they say my name funny as if the syllables were made out of tin and hurt the roof of your mouth. But in Spanish my name is made out of a softer something, like silver, not quite as thick as sister's name Magdalena--which is uglier than mine. Magdalena who at least–can come home and become Nenny. But I am always Esperanza. I would like to baptize myself under a new name, a name more like the real me, the one nobody sees. Esperanza as Lisandra or Maritza or Zeze the X. Yes. Something like Zeze the X will do.

During Writing

Invite students to write their own narrative of My Name. For students who know very little about their names such as why their parents picked that name or what their name

CHAPTER 1

means, they can focus on how they feel about their names or write a series of questions about their name instead.

After Writing

If students' narratives are long, invite a few students to share their writing. The teacher may also invite students to read one line of their choosing, creating a collage of new material from familiar faces in the classroom.

Sharing Student Writing

> I got my name from my father's side of the family. The oral tradition in my family is that my great-great grandfather's life was saved by the Indian chief of the Kalusa Indian tribe, probably in Florida during or shortly after the American civil war. In honour of the chief, he named his daughter KlooLoo (which was his translation). Thereafter, the name was passed down to all of the daughters. The last woman in the family to have the name as a first name was my great grandmother. I framed her wedding invitation from 1913.
>
> -Kloo

> My name is Sarah. My grandmother's name is Sarah Elizabeth but she has always gone by Liz and she can't tell you why. I always thought it common, like a beat you hear over and over; nothing new or exciting. I always thought my name made me plain. As I've grown, I feel pride in sharing my name with my grandmother, the most non-plain person I know.
>
> -Sarah

> *Gone With The Wind* was one of the first American movies my Austrian-born mother saw as a teenager. The interest stuck and that's how I became Scarlett. But negative feedback from strangers unhinged my mother's confidence. One month before my 1st birthday, my mother added the name Rebecca. Change came quickly. A new birth certificate was issued, the original destroyed and thin white stickers covered up handwritten Scarletts carefully written in my baby book. Scarlett was even erased from my ID bracelet and polished over with Rebecca. Looking closely, the letters 'S' and 't' still remain as a faint reminder. In high school, I peeled off those stickers.
>
> -Scarlett

REFERENCES

Christensen, L. (2000). *Reading, writing, and rising up: Teaching about social justice and the power of the written word.* Milwaukee: WI: Rethinking Schools.
Cisneros, S. (1984). *The house on mango street.* New York, NY: Vintage.

THIS I BELIEVE

Editors Jay Allison and Dan Gediman's (2006; 2008) *This I Believe* and *This I Believe II* in association with National Public Radio (NPR) is a collection of belief-narratives from the famous (e.g., Bill Gates) to the unknown (e.g., a man who serves on Rhode Island's parole board). Each piece is different, the writing personal and engaging. I like to share these narratives with students because they compel them to think deeply about their own personal beliefs – about writing, teaching, family – about anything that matters to them.

Before Writing

Begin a discussion with students on their beliefs. What beliefs do they hold dear? What life experiences inform their beliefs? Next, read the following two selections from *This I Believe*.

> I believe that everyone deserves flowers on their grave. When I go to the cemetery to visit my brother, it makes me sad to see graves – just the cold stones – and no flowers on them. They look lonely, like nobody loves them. I believe this is the worst thing in the world – that loneliness. No one to visit you and brush off the dust from your name and cover you with colour. A grave without any flowers looks like the person has been forgotten. And then what was the point of even living – to be forgotten? (p. 16)

> I believe in the ingredients of love, the elements from which it is made. I believe in love's humble, practical components and their combined power (p. 144).

During Writing

Invite students to write their own paragraph of This I Believe. Rather than write a series of belief statements, encourage students to choose one and develop it into a moving and stirring piece.

After Writing

Invite a few students to share their writing. The teacher may also invite all students to share just one line from their writing. Students can say, "Pass" if they do not want to share.

Sharing Student Writing

> I believe that family is everything.
> I believe love is thicker than skin.

CHAPTER 1

> When everything is upside down,
> family turns you right side up.
> When all else fails,
> family never fails you. This I believe.
>   -Lauren

I believe we all fear what we don't understand. Those who appreciate their fears are the only unique souls who can change their judgment into understanding, compassion, and love.
This I believe.
   -Sarah

I believe there will always be change.
I believe things do not always turn out as expected.
I believe in my parents' love for me.
I do not believe in much right now.
I want to believe life will get better.
I want to believe in God, his love for me.
And in my grandma, that she's still looking out for me.
Please help me believe.
   -Whitney

REFERENCES

Allison, J., & Gediman, D. (2006). *This I believe: The personal philosophies of remarkable men and women.* New York, NY: Henry Holt.

Allison, J., & Gediman, D. (2008). *This I believe II: The personal philosophies of remarkable men and women.* New York, NY: Henry Holt.

I REMEMBER

Joe Brainard's (2001) *I Remember* is a collection of reflections and remembrances that each begin with the refrain, "I remember." They range from the funny to the serious and offer a collage of images of American life. I like to share these one-liners with students because the writing is honest and each line is a potential story, waiting to be written. A beautiful story can emerge from a single reflection. It is important that students access their own reflections to see the abundance of stories that exist within each of them.

Before Writing

Begin a discussion on memories. Which memories do you hold dear? Which memories feel more like nightmares? Which sensory details (e.g., taste, touch, smell, sound, see) stand out the most to you? Next, read selected lines from Brainard's (2001) book.

> I remember how good a glass of water can taste after a dish of ice cream (p. 8).
> I remember Aunt Cleora who lived in Hollywood. Every year for Christmas she sent my brother and me a joint present of one book (p. 13).
> I remember my grade school art teacher, Mrs. Chick, who got so mad at a boy one day she dumped a bucket of water over his head (p. 15).
> I remember many first days of school. And that empty feeling (p. 17).
> I remember when I thought that if you did anything bad, policemen would put you in jail (p. 20).
> I remember taffeta. And the way it sounded (p. 23).
> I remember making a cross of two sticks for something my brother and me buried. It might have been a cat but I think it was a bug or something (p. 43).
> I remember rearranging boxes of candy so it would look like not so much was missing (p. 45).
> I remember the first time I saw the ocean. I jumped right in, and it swept me right under, down, and back to shore again (p. 51).
> I remember screen doors that slam. And "You're letting in the flies" (p. 79).
> I remember the only time I ever saw my mother cry. I was eating apricot pie (p. 105).

During Writing

Invite students to write their own list of I Remember statements. Once they are done, ask students to put a star beside the memories they think are worth writing about and then choose one I remember line to develop further. Remind students to include some sensory details in their writing.

CHAPTER 1

After Writing

Invite a few students to read their I Remember narrative. If time is limited, several students can share one line around the room.

Sharing Student Writing

> I remember having chicken pox. Twice.
> I remember streets before they became cement. (*)
> I remember sneaking finger dabs of powdered sugar when my mother wasn't looking.
> I remember screaming at the top of my lungs when I watched a snake slither out of the garden hose, my summer drinking water source.

> *I remember streets before they became cement, when they were narrow and rocky and covered you in a veil of dust. One summer, I met Andrew standing in his yard. There we were, staring at each other on either side of a dirt road with pebbles in our shoes. We had the same look. We knew what we were doing to do: tear down the road in our first bike duel. He was 5; I was 6. Twenty years later, we still ride those streets together, only now they are wider and smoother.
>   -Amber

REFERENCE

Brainard, J. (2001). *I remember.* New York, NY: Granary Books.

THE INVITATION

Canadian writer Oriah Mountain Dreamer's (1999) *The Invitation* is a free verse poem about relationships. I like to share this poem with students because the repeating lines, "It doesn't interest me," and "I want to know" speak honestly and openly about matters of the heart that students can practice in their own writing. Specifically, The Invitation invites "the writer to show his cards" (Ravitch, 1984, p. 7) about what he/she believes is core or essential about the human heart.

Before Writing

Begin a discussion on relationships. Ask students to think about what does/does not interest them about someone else. What do they think is essential in a relationship? Ask students to imagine writing to someone they know. What questions do they have for them? How do these questions relate to the human heart? Next, read Oriah's The Invitation.

> It doesn't interest me
> what you do for a living.
> I want to know
> what you ache for
> and if you dare to dream
> of meeting your heart's longing.
> It doesn't interest me
> how old you are.
> I want to know
> if you will risk
> looking like a fool
> for love
> for your dream
> for the adventure of being alive.
> It doesn't interest me
> what planets are
> squaring your moon...
> I want to know
> if you have touched
> the centre of your own sorrow
> if you have been opened
> by life's betrayals
> or have become shrivelled and closed
> from fear of further pain.
> I want to know
> if you can sit with pain

CHAPTER 1

mine or your own
without moving to hide it
or fade it
or fix it.
I want to know
if you can be with joy
mine or your own
if you can dance with wildness
and let the ecstasy fill you
to the tips of your fingers and toes
without cautioning us
to be careful
to be realistic
to remember the limitations
of being human.
It doesn't interest me
if the story you are telling me
is true.
I want to know if you can
disappoint another
to be true to yourself.
If you can bear
the accusation of betrayal
and not betray your own soul.
If you can be faithless
and therefore trustworthy.
I want to know if you can see Beauty
even when it is not pretty
every day.
And if you can source your own life
from its presence.
I want to know
if you can live with failure
yours and mine
and still stand at the edge of the lake
and shout to the silver of the full moon,
"Yes."
It doesn't interest me
to know where you live
or how much money you have.
I want to know if you can get up
after the night of grief and despair
weary and bruised to the bone

and do what needs to be done
to feed the children.
It doesn't interest me
who you know
or how you came to be here.
I want to know if you will stand
in the centre of the fire
with me
and not shrink back.
It doesn't interest me
where or what or with whom
you have studied.
I want to know
what sustains you
from the inside
when all else falls away.
I want to know
if you can be alone
with yourself
and if you truly like
the company you keep
in the empty moments.

During Writing

Invite students to write their own Invitation poem or narrative. If writing a poem, they can write in free verse or any poem structure they feel comfortable using. Once they are done, ask students to put a star beside the "It doesn't interest me" lines and the "I want to know" lines they think are the most telling statements about their invitation.

After Writing

Invite students to share just two lines: One "It doesn't interest me" line; and one, "I want to know" line.

Sharing Student Writing

It doesn't interest me how much money you have in the bank. I want to know if you would give everything you had for just one more minute with the one you lost. It doesn't interest me who you give thanks and praise to every night when the moon shines. I want to know if you will love unconditionally, if you

CHAPTER 1

will forgive others even when it hurts. I want to know if you will stand tall by my side no matter the forecast in life. It doesn't interest me how strong you are physically. I want to know if you are strong enough mentally. I want to know if you are able to see the silver lining when life throws a curve ball. I want to know if you will see the curve ball as an opportunity that will help make you a better person.

    -Cory

REFERENCES

http://www.oriahmountaindreamer.com
Oriah. (1999). *The invitation*. San Francisco, CA: HarperOne.
Ravitch, D. (1984). Reviving the craft of writing. *College Board Review, 132*, 4–8.

CHAPTER 2

JOYFUL NONSENSE

FUNNY AND UNFUNNY WORDS

Art Peterson's (1996) *The Writer's Workout Book: 113 Stretches Toward Better Prose* offers a formidable collection of writing ideas through several themed chapters. "Know the Difference Between Funny and Unfunny Words" (p. 197) is a list writing exercise that calls on students to think of word pairs and their images and decide which are funny and not funny. I like to share this list with students because it encourages visualization of people, places, and objects and requires attention to sounds of words and how pronunciation affects meaning.

Before Writing

Begin a discussion with students on words that make them laugh and words that do not. What makes a word funny, silly, or goofy? What words do they consider serious, grave, or deep? Why do mental images matter when choosing words? How does the way certain words sound when spoken out loud factor into making a funny/unfunny list? Finally, read, "Know the Difference Between Funny and Unfunny Words." Make a copy of this list so that students can see them on a white board, smart board, or overhead projector.

Not Funny	*Funny*
England	Liechtenstein
Tights	Pantyhose
Oil	Gas
Science Diet	Kibbles n Bits
Jeopardy	Let's Make a Deal
April 15	April 1
Tomato	Rutabaga
Astronomy	Astrology
Latin	Pig Latin
Harvard	Chico State
MLK Day	Groundhog Day

CHAPTER 2

During Writing

Invite students to write their own list of Funny And Unfunny Words. Like Peterson's, students' word lists can deal with many topics or focus on one idea (e.g., funny/unfunny fruits; funny/unfunny meals; funny/unfunny games, etc.). Some students may prefer to work in pairs.

After Writing

If working in pairs, invite each pair to share two examples from their lists.

Sharing Student Writing

Safe Sex	Prophylactics
Volley ball	Dodge ball
Rib eye Steak	Chicken Fried Steak
Professional	Gifted Amateur
Mini dress	Booty cutter
Complaining	Kvetching
Precocious	Mannish
Fledgling	Newbie
Plague	Scourge
Depressive	Debbie Downer

   -Sheila

Noisemaker	Kazoo
Necktie	Ascot
Monkey	Lemur
Animals	Critters
Scrub Brush	Loofa
Eggs	Quiche

   -Nate

Orange	Kiwi
Olive	Pickle
Feta	Gorgonzola
Beef Stroganoff	Boeuf Bourguignon
Soda	Pop

   -Scarlett

REFERENCE

Peterson, A. (1996). *The writer's workout book: 113 stretches toward better prose.* Berkeley, CA: National.

JOYFUL NONSENSE

TEN MEMBERS

I cannot recall in which book I came across "Ten Members of a Class or Species" that included seventeen-year-old Ken Skidmore's classification of 10 kinds of trees. But I like to share this list with students because it is a natural phenomenon to group ideas and it allows students to show their knowledge on a particular subject of personal interest.

Before Writing

Begin a discussion with students on groups of things that they know a lot about. Some of these ideas may be gender specific (e.g., purses, make-up, running shoes, and Sunday sports) or generic (e.g., birds, dogs, national monuments, top holiday destinations). Finally, read Skidmore's list of trees.

   Elmer
   Pineton
   Barkman
   Twiggie
   Leafy
   Woody
   Stub
   Stumper
   Woodstalk
   Oakley

During Writing

Invite students to write their own Ten Members list of a class or species.

After Writing

Invite students to share two or three words from their lists. Begin a discussion on how some of these words might be used in personal narrative writing (e.g., names of characters or places, story titles).

Sharing Student Writing

   An Incredibly Biased List of the 10 Best Beatles Songs
   10. Can't Buy Me Love
   9. Come Together
   8. You Never Give Me Your Money/Golden Slumbers/The End
   7. Lady Madonna

49

CHAPTER 2

    8. Ticket to Ride
    6. Something
    5. Lucy in the Sky with Diamonds
    4. You've Got to Hide Your Love Away
    3. Here Comes the Sun
    2. Paperback Writer
    1. Ob-La-Di, Ob-La-Dah
        -Bridget

10 different styles of Waffle House Hash Browns
-Smothered (w/onions)
-Covered (w/melted cheese)
-Topped (w/chili)
-Diced (w/tomatoes)
-Chunked (w/ham)
-Quarter plate (hamburger w/hash browns)
-Peppered (w/peppers)
-Capped (w/mushrooms)
-Scattered (not contained in cooking ring)
-Well done (my favourite!)
        -Scott

GOOD BAND NAMES FOR MY BAND
Coffin Birth
The Ligatures
In Broad Daylight
Foot Stool
Meat Wash
Blunt Force Trauma
Organs 4 Sale
Risk & Reward
Blood Snake
The Ticking Time Bombs
        -Scottoosh

DO'S AND DON'TS

Todd Parr's (2004) *Do's and Don'ts* is a board picture book that shows contrasting ideas through simple and sometimes humorous text (e.g., I do brush my teeth after every meal; I don't brush with peanut butter). I like to share this book with students because it inspired me to write "Being Canadian: Do's and Don'ts." It is important that students can see how a simple writing structure such as that found in Parr's book could be used to inspire unique, and potentially complex, writing topics.

Before Writing

Begin a discussion on rules. For example, what rules do they know from their childhood? Adolescence? Adulthood? Friendships and/or relationships? Having a part-time job? Having a pet? Inspired by Parr's book, I wrote a do's and don'ts list about being Canadian. Begin a discussion on how this writing engagement can be used to express humour and seriousness in writing.

Do speed in kilometers	Don't speed in miles
Do contact your Premier	Don't contact your Governor
Do say Prime Minister	Don't say President
Do say chocolate bar	Don't say candy bar
Do say pop	Don't say soda
Do say 16 Celsius	Don't say 61 Fahrenheit
Do say zed	Don't say zee
Do order salami in grams	Don't order salami in pounds
Do order Tortière	Don't order shepherd's pie
Do wear a toque	Don't wear a beanie
Do spell colour with a U	Don't spell colour like this: color
Do write on foolscap	Don't write on legal paper
Do write a cheque	Don't write a check
Do eat at Tim Hortons	Don't eat at Krispycreme or Dunkin' Donuts
Do eat wagon wheels	Don't eat moon pies
Do eat ketchup potato chips	Don't eat plain chips
Do eat pea meal bacon	Don't eat Canadian Bacon
Do ask for the washroom	Don't ask for the bathroom
Do pay with a Loonie	Don't pay with a dollar bill
Do drink at 19	Don't drink at 21
Do avoid the RCMP	Don't avoid the FBI
Do pump gas in litres	Don't pump gas in gallons
Do count your provinces	Don't count your states
Do ask for a postal code	Don't ask for a zip code

CHAPTER 2

During Writing

Invite students to write their own list of Do's And Don'ts. They may write as little as five or as many as twenty. Lists can have a theme (e.g., wedding) or include a mixture of unrelated ideas.

After Writing

Once students have finished writing, invite individual students to share one do/don't line, or more if time permits.

Sharing Student Writing

Do flush	Don't let it mellow
Do sneeze in elbow	Don't sneeze on people
Do say thank you	Don't feel entitled
Do knock before entering	Don't just walk in
Do show empathy	Don't be insensitive
Do pick up after yourself	Don't expect others to be your Mom
Do be socially gracious	Don't be a social embarrassment
Do visit friends	Don't wear out your welcome
Do bring a house-warming gift	Don't take hospitality for granted
Do take the high road	Don't repay evil with evil

   -Sheila

Do cut your guest list	Don't invite your 3rd cousin
Do set the date	Don't push it back
Do use peonies	Don't use daises
Do eat brunch	Don't eat dinner
Do find your dress alone	Don't bring the world
Do set a budget	Don't fiddle with the plans
Do get a ring	Don't get ahead of yourself

   -Alisha

Do bring your own gear	Don't borrow
Do dress up; it's a Renaissance Fair	Don't dress like a *Storm Trooper*
Do wear comfortable shoes	Don't wear sunglasses
Do respect all participants	Don't assume a girl 5'2"can't knock you flat. Ouch.
Do try different equipment & styles	Don't paint *Hello Kitty* on your shield
Do be prepared to wrestle a little	Don't try to tackle a guy in metal armor

Do expect full-contact fighting	Don't assume a sword made of foam doesn't hurt
Do have lots of fun	Don't take Dagorhir *too seriously*

-Nate, *who participates in Dagorhir (a Medieval Combat Reenactment society).*

REFERENCE

Parr, T. (2004). *Do's and Don'ts*. New York, NY: Little Brown & Co.

CHAPTER 2

FORTUNATELY

Remy Charlip's (1964) *Fortunately* is a picture book about a boy named Ned who experiences obstacles in his travels. The tale is told through a series of fortunate and unfortunate events where colour is thoughtfully used (e.g., colourful pages for fortunate events and black and white pages for unfortunate events) to show ridiculous and extraordinary happenings. I like to share this book with students because fortunate/unfortunate events can be light-hearted or downright serious.

Before Writing

Begin a discussion on fortunate and unfortunate events. Ask students to reflect on one or two events in their own lives that felt fortunate/unfortunate. Encourage students to describe these experiences. For example, are they amusing, silly, sad, or serious? Students may also tailor this discussion around global events. Next, read *Fortunately*.

> Fortunately one day, Ned got a letter that said, "Please Come to a Surprise Party."
> But unfortunately the party was in Florida and he was in New York.
> Fortunately, a friend loaned him an airplane.
> Unfortunately the motor exploded.
> Fortunately there was a parachute in the airplane.
> Unfortunately there was a hole in the parachute.
> Fortunately there was a haystack on the ground.
> Unfortunately, there was a pitchfork in the haystack.
> Fortunately he missed the pitchfork.
> Unfortunately he missed the haystack.
> Fortunately he landed in water.
> Unfortunately there were sharks in the water.
> Fortunately he could swim.
> Unfortunately there were tigers on the land.
> Fortunately he could run.
> Unfortunately he ran into a deep dark cave.
> Fortunately he could dig.
> Unfortunately he dug himself into a fancy ballroom.
> Fortunately there was a surprise party going on. And fortunately the party was for him, because fortunately it was his birthday!

During Writing

Invite students to write their own narrative of Fortunately. They may choose a funny topic to write about or a serious one.

After Writing

Invite one of two students to share their narratives. Once the stories have been shared, peers may offer suggestions for story titles, a departure from Charlip's one-word title, *Fortunately*.

Sharing Student Writing

> Fortunately, the other day I met the most beautiful girl I've ever seen.
> Unfortunately, she was the ER nurse who helped set my broken arm.
> Fortunately, the doctor said the break was pretty minor.
> Unfortunately, I still had to stay for a few days.
> Fortunately, I didn't miss any days of class.
> Unfortunately, when I got back home I'd lost my keys!
> Fortunately, I was able to borrow my mom's car.
> Unfortunately, it ran out of gas halfway to school.
> Fortunately, a man offered me a lift.
> Unfortunately, it was in the rumble seat of his Model A.
> Fortunately, we didn't have a long way to go.
> Unfortunately, we never got there.
> Fortunately, the guys who jacked the car let me keep my wallet.
> Unfortunately, they took all my money so I couldn't pay the bus fare.
> Um, that's why I'm late to class today, Professor…
>
>   -Nate

> Fortunately, we planned a vacation to Las Vegas.
> Unfortunately our friends had to travel across nine time zones.
> Fortunately, they had business class seats.
> Unfortunately, I wore a hair weave in 105-degree heat.
> Fortunately, everywhere we went there was air conditioning.
> Unfortunately, our German friends didn't like air conditioning.
> Fortunately, we all liked *Blue Man Group* and *Cirque du Soleil*.
> Unfortunately, the food at Emeril's was not as good as I had fantasized.
> Fortunately, the food, service, and decor at *Le Cirque* far exceeded my fantasies.
> Unfortunately, the whole experience left one friend in tears from exhaustion.
> Fortunately, we all enjoyed being together at *Disney World* with fangs.
>
>   -Sheila

REFERENCE

Charlip, R. (1964). *Fortunately*. New York, NY: Simon & Schuster.

CHAPTER 2

PREFERENCES

Jeff Kinney's (2008) "Your Desert Island Picks" (p. 2) in *Diary of a Wimpy Kid Do-It-Yourself Book* inspired "Preferences" in which students list generic things (e.g., ice cream) followed by a comma and their preference to that word (e.g., mint chocolate chip). I like to share my list of preferences with students because while it gives them a Birdseye view of my likes/dislikes, writing their own list allows them to experience specificity in their writing.

Before Writing

Begin a discussion on preferences, such as a kind of ice cream or a brand of shoe. Next, invite students to volunteer general topics (e.g., milk, movie, pillows, art, actress, chocolate, song, dinner, peanut butter, team, cookie, flower, instrument, jeans, computer, dog, music, TV show, dessert, car, actor, holiday, tree, restaurant, bling) and write them down on a whiteboard, blackboard, or smart board, to keep the conversation going. Write a comma after each idea, followed by a preference. Finally, read my list of preferences to students.

   Colour, green and blue (in that order)
   Water, no ice thank you
   Pillows, fluffy
   Sour cream, the real thing
   Doughnut, sprinkles please
   Movies, drama
   Language, French
   Tea, Mandarin Orchard & English Breakfast
   Chocolate, dark with orange (please, oh please)
   Wine, Valpolicella
   Pet, dog for sure
   Art, watercolour
   Instrument, piano
   Flowers, red tulips and pink roses (Hydrangea, too)
   Cookie, any kind
   Room spray, citrus
   Ice cream, never chocolate
   Peanut butter, never ever

During Writing

Invite students to write their own list of Preferences. Students' preferences may include a range of ideas or focus on one idea (e.g., all movie preferences that include examples of action, drama, suspense/thriller, horror, comedy, romance, mystery, documentary, science fiction, crime, animation, fantasy, and family).

After Writing

Students may share three or four of their preferences. This sharing may prompt discussion of shared favourites in the classroom (e.g. who else likes vanilla ice cream?), which can promote a sense of community.

Sharing Student Writing

    M&M's, Peanut
    Travel, National Parks
    Computer, MAC (even though I can't afford one)
    Cell phone, No Internet
    Colour, Orange
    Music, P!nk
        -Laura

    Scotch, 18 year old
    Men, Intelligent and funny
    Celebrity, Overrated
    Ethnic Food, Mexican Tamales
    Wine, White Bordeaux
    Tea. Real please. Earl Grey
    Dogs, Chihuahuas
    Doctors, Talkative
    Friends, Authentic
    Vacation, Deserted beach
        -Sheila

    Colour, Purple
    Water, Sparkling
    Music, Alternative
    Sushi, White tuna
    Soda, Coke
    Dancing, Wild
    Outdoors, Camping
    Flowers, Columbine
        -Alison

REFERENCE

Kinney, J. (2008). *Diary of a wimpy kid do-it-yourself book.* New York, NY: Amulet Books.

CHAPTER 2

COURAGE

Bernard Waber's (2002) *Courage* is a picture book about courage, from the simple to the extraordinary. I like to share this book with students because it offers them realistic examples of what every-day-courage looks and feels like. Waber's honest writing also encourages students to reflect on what courage means to them and write about it.

Before Writing

Begin a discussion on courage. What does courage mean to us? What does it mean to have courage? What are some examples of courage? Next, read Bernard Waber's (2002) picture book titled *Courage*. Though the illustrations are cartoonish and simple, the examples of courage are broad and reach many ages. Readers of all ages will enjoy the images Waber used to help visually express courage.

> There are many kinds of courage.
> Awesome kinds.
> And everyday kinds.
> Still, courage is courage – whatever kind.
> Courage is riding your bicycle for the first time without training wheels.
> Courage is a spelling bee and your word is superciliousness.
> Courage is two candy bars and saving one for tomorrow.
> Courage is mealtime and desperately hoping it's not Chunky Chunks in "real" gravy again.
> Courage is nobody better pick on your little brother.
> Courage is it's your job to check out the night noises in the house.
> Courage is being the new kid on the block and saying flat out, "Hi, my name is Wayne. What's yours?"
> Courage is tasting the vegetable before making a face.
> Courage is not peeking at the last pages of your whodunit book to find out who did it.
> Courage is being the first to make up after an argument.
> Courage is deliberately stepping on sidewalk cracks.
> Courage is the juicy secret you promised never to tell.
> Courage is the bottom of the ninth, tie score, two outs, bases loaded, and your turn to bat.
> Courage is being sudsed and scrubbed by strangers.
> Courage is breaking bad habits.
> Courage is suddenly remembering a silly joke and trying not to giggle when everyone else is being especially serious.
> Courage is arriving much too early for a birthday party.

Courage is sending a valentine to someone you secretly admire, and signing your real name.
Courage is going to bed without a nightlight.
Courage is admiring, but not plucking.
Courage is deciding to have your hair cut.
Courage is trying to cover up your mean, jealous side.
Courage is a scenic car trip and being struck in the middle during the best part,
Courage is explaining the rip in your brand-new pants.
Courage is going on it again.
Courage is if you knew where there were some mountains, you would definitely climb them.
Courage is exploring heights.
Courage is a blade of grass breaking through the icy snow.
Courage is starting over.
Courage is holding on to your dream.
Courage is being a firefighter, or a police officer.
Courage is sometimes having to say goodbye.
Courage is what we give to each other.

During Writing

Invite students to write their own list of Courage. Ask them, "What does courage mean to you? What does it feel and look like?" Tell students that they cannot use examples from the book. Rather, encourage students to write examples that are unique and fresh.

After Writing

Ask students to star/circle one courage statement from their lists that they want to share. To avoid repetition of shared ideas, tell students that this statement should be the most unique. Students can popcorn these courage statements until everyone around the room has had the opportunity to share.

Sharing Student Writing

> Courage is running your first 5K race.
> Courage is standing up for what you believe in, especially when you are alone.
> Courage is fighting cancer.
> Courage is getting into the lake when you know it is cold.
> Courage is loving your puppy after he has eaten your favourite pair of shoes.
> Courage is saying no.
>   -Michelle

CHAPTER 2

> Courage is flying across the world. Alone.
> -DePorre

> Courage is being strong enough to tell you I am not ready.
> -Lauren

> Courage is talking to an upset parent.
> -Rebecca

> Courage is letting yourself feel grief.
> Courage is dreaming big.
> -Sarah

REFERENCE

Waber, B. (2002). *Courage*. New York, NY: Houghton Mifflin.

EQUATIONS FOR LIVING

Craig Damrauer's (2006) *New Math: Equations for Living* is a trade book that includes simple life equations told through a mathematical lens. I like to share this book with students because it combines two modes of communication, math and writing, and encourages students to apply their understanding of math literacy through language.

Before Writing

Begin a discussion on how simple math equations (e.g., 2 x 2 = 4), when replaced with language, (e.g., Pretty x Pretty = Gorgeous) can communicate ideas. With grade level in mind, which equations to discuss in class (e.g., addition, subtraction, division, multiplication, exponents) will vary from classroom to classroom. Read several equations from *New Math: Equations for Living* to stimulate discussion about blending math and language vocabulary to communicate some life equations. Older students with more math experiences may appreciate some of the subtler equations and enjoy discussing the significance of signs in how they carry meaning (e.g., Does LOVE=LIKE X LIKE mean the same as LOVE=LIKE + LIKE?).

ANGER= TICKED OFF[3]
HAPPY=UNHAPPY-UN
CRAZY=TALKING TO ONESELF-(CELL PHONE + EAR PIECE)
RAISIN=GRAPE+TIME
DOGGIE DAY CARE=KENNEL-GUILT
LOVE=LIKE X LIKE
PATERNITY=WHAT? + ARE YOU SURE?
SANTA CLAUS=THE TOOTH FAIRY+250LBS
MIME=JUGGLER-BALLS
MODERN ART=I COULD DO THAT+YEAH, BUT YOU DIDN'T
VALUE=PERCEPTION X TIME

During Writing

Invite students to write their own Equations For Living. Ask them, "What life equations are essential to you?" Students may diversify their life equations (e.g., addition, subtraction, and multiplication) or focus on one kind of equation (e.g., addition only). Students may also prefer to write themed equations (e.g., Equations for Living with Five Brothers).

CHAPTER 2

After Writing

Invite students to share a couple of equations. This sharing may be grouped by listening to humorous examples, serious examples, ironic examples, witty examples, etc.

Sharing Student Writing

SUMMER = (SPRING + HUMIDITY) X FUN
    -Krystin

SUMMER HAIR = ME-THE BLOW DRYER
    -Alana

REREADING = REVELING + READING
    -Sarah

FRIENDSHIP = (TRUST + UNDERSTANDING) - JEALOUSY
    -Danielle

REFERENCE

Damrauer, C. (2006). *New math: Equations for living.* Kansas City, MO: Andrews McMeel.

TAKE A BREATH

Art Peterson's (1996) *The Writer's Workout Book: 113 Stretches Toward Better Prose* offers a formidable collection of writing ideas through several themed chapters. "Take a Breath" (p. 12) lists substances, objects, and animals that produce odour. I like to share this list with students because as they think about odours, they are called to think about how sensory details in writing can be used to make odours more vivid and descriptive.

Before Writing

Begin a discussion on substances, objects, and animals that produce odour. Which odours do we like and loathe? First responses may be simple (e.g., hair) but nudge students to be specific (e.g., wet dog hair) when describing the odour. Next, read the column of word examples from *Take a Breath* in Art Peterson's (1996) *The Writer's Workout Book: 113 Stretches Toward Better Prose.* Ask students to improve upon Peterson's list. Two-week old garbage, for example, mentally conjures different odour than, say, just garbage.

Sea air	Wet wool	Disinfectant
Wood	Marijuana	Dogs
Cat boxes	Old milk	Hairspray
Fresh laundry	Soap	Grass
Incense	Skunks	Garbage
Garlic	Chili	Popcorn
Leather	New books	New cars
Whiskey	Candles	Pine needles
Coffee	Tobacco smoke	Sewage
Feet	French Fries	

During Writing

Invite students to write their own Take A Breath, to make a list of things (e.g., animals, substances, objects) that produce odour. Remind students that specificity in writing helps create mental images for readers.

After Writing

Invite students to share their lists in small groups first to avoid sharing repeated ideas with the whole group. Then ask students to choose the most unique from their odour causing lists and share with the whole group.

CHAPTER 2

Sharing Student Writing

Milky vomit	Mildew	Cut lemons
Barbecue	Baked apple pie	Moth balls
Baby Powder	Bleach	Chlorine
Nail Polish	Brand new tires	Tennis balls
-Dani		
Babies	Musty hair	Summer rain
Coffee brewing	Musty basements	Teenage boys
Morning breath	Vinegar	Sunscreen
-Jessica		
Steamed Brussels Sprouts	Dog breath	Dog farts
-Susan		
Squeezed lemon	Fried onions and bacon	Sea air
Sugar beets in the fall	Fresh basil	Orange zest
Mint	Cinnamon baked apples	Dried sweat
Newborns	Fresh strawberries	Sour milk
Week-old diapers	Feminine hygiene products	Dead fish
-Sheila		

REFERENCE

Peterson, A. (1996). *The writer's workout book: 113 stretches toward better prose.* Berkeley, CA: National Writing Project.

JOYFUL NONSENSE

FAMILY FEUD

Family Feud is an American television game show where two unrelated families compete against each other to name the most popular answers to survey questions posed to one hundred people. I like to share some of the survey questions with students because while they typically garner a lot of laughter while writing, they nudge students to think about what they know on a given topic.

Before Writing

Begin a discussion with students on words they know that all begin with the same word (e.g., chicken coop, chicken soup, etc.). Read the following three game show examples.

Chicken Coop	Airborne	Hangman
Chicken Little	Airplane	Hang ten
Chicken Pot Pie	Airport	Hangnail
Chicken Nuggets	Air Jordan	Hang on
Chicken Soup	Air freshener	Hang up
Chicken Fingers	Air conditioning	Hangover
Chicken Salad	Air ball	Hang tight
	Airtight	

During Writing

Invite students to write their own Family Feud word list by starting with words they know that start with 'open' and 'under' or words that have the word 'captain' in them. The English language makes certain there are endless possibilities here!

After Writing

Invite students to share one word from their lists and then invite the rest of the class to add words not mentioned.

Sharing Student Writing

Dog tired	Chicken breast
Dog eared	Chicken thigh
Dogged	Chicken drumstick
Doggone	Chicken potpie
Dog bone	Chicken à la king
Dog house	Chicken noodle soup
Doggy	Chicken tortilla coup

CHAPTER 2

  Dogfish   Chicken lemon rice soup
  Dog-eat-dog   Chicken Parmesan
  Dog's life   Chicken Marsala
  Dogma   Chicken sausage
  Dog paddle   Chicken stock
  Dogwood   Chicken sandwich
  Dog watch   Chicken feed
  Dog catcher   Chicken egg
  Dog days   Grilled chicken
  Dog food   Fried chicken
  Dog and pony show Headless chicken
  Dog fight
            -Patricia
    -Sheila

REFERENCE

Goodson, M., & Todman, B. (Producers). (2012). *Family Feud* [Television series]. Hollywood: American Broadcasting Company.

FANTASTIC BINOMIALS

Gianni Rodari's (1996) *The Grammar of Fantasy: An Introduction to the Art of Inventing Stories* is a book about imaginative writing exercises that includes "The Fantastic Binomial" among many others used in the schools of Reggio Emilia in northern Italy. "Fantastic Binomials" involves creating unique word combinations. I like to share binomials with students because extraordinary story possibilities are possible by simply juxtaposing two unique ideas (e.g., dog and closet), which creates distance between the words, making them fantastic or interesting.

Before Writing

Begin a discussion on how words, when paired together, can conjure up mental images of unique ideas. Invite students to share some nouns and write these words in a two-column list on a whiteboard, blackboard, or smart board. Next, draw lines to match words from one column to the other to create unique word combinations. "Horse-dog," explains Rodari (p. 12), is not a fantastic binomial because the zoological classification is the same. There must be some distance between the two words in order for the combination to be a fantastic binomial (e.g., "dog-closet"). Distance creates a condition for generating a story, where a binomial should feel like a discovery or an invention. Select a binomial that conjures up unique story potential and rewrite the binomial four or more ways with various prepositions (e.g., as, at, but, by, down, for, from, in, into, like, near, next, of, off, on, onto, out, over, past, plus, minus, since, than, to, up, with). Finally, read Rodari's example.

> The dog with the closet;
> The closet of the dog;
> The dog in the closet; or
> The dog on the closet. (p. 13)

During Writing

Invite students to work in pairs and co-write Fantastic Binomials by first generating a two-column list. Together, students can create fantastic binomials by matching words from their lists. Once their list is complete, ask students to select one binomial, rewrite with prepositions, and circle the prepositional binomial that they believe has the greatest story potential. Time permitting, students may begin co-authoring their story.

After Writing

Invite students to share one fantastic binomial that they agree holds the greatest story potential. Also invite to share those who may have begun developing a story from their binomial.

CHAPTER 2

Sharing Student Writing

>Sprinkles on the unicorn;
>Sprinkles in the unicorn;
>Sprinkles under the unicorn;
>Sprinkles atop unicorns;
>Sprinkles throughout unicorn valley;
>Unicorns with sprinkles; or
>Unicorns from sprinkles.
>   -Sarah

REFERENCE

Rodari, G. (1996). *The grammar of fantasy: An introduction to the art of inventing stories.* New York, NY: Teachers and Writers Collaborative.

SPOONERISMS

Carter and Denton's (2009) *Orange Silver Sausage: A Collection of Poems without Rhymes* is a collection of fifty non-rhyming poems that range in silliness including Andy Seed's "The Rev Spooner's Shopping List" (p. 19). This quirky list concerns spoonerisms, a play on words (named after Reverend Spooner) where consonants and vowels are deliberately switched for a humorous effect. I like to share spoonerisms with students because they explore humour in writing. As well, through very simple but humorous word play, students can discover potential story titles or topics for quirky stories.

Before Writing

Begin a discussion on neologisms, words, terms, or phrases that are newly coined by an individual or group of people and sometimes share common meaning, especially if they develop from a particular event or public occasion. Continue the discussion that spoonerisms, much like neologisms, are also newly coined and invented words. Invite students to volunteer words and write them down on a whiteboard, blackboard, or smart board so that everyone can see them. This call for words can be random and therefore broad or specific (e.g., What are some of your favourite foods or snacks? What games do you like to play?), which orients students' thinking about a possible response. Two words work best (e.g., Happy Days) since it is easier to see which letters need to be switched. Next, deliberately switch first consonants or vowels. Depending on the word, it may be easy to step up the silliness of the engagement by switching the first two consonants or vowels. Finally, read Andy Seed's "The Rev Spooner's Shopping List".

- Jaspberry ram
- Chot hocolate
- Ninger guts
- Beggie vurger
- Sea poup
- Spixed mice
- Lairy fiquid
- Bea tags
- Pushroom mizza
- Chini meddars
- Jackcurrant belly
- Poo laper
- Nicken choodles
- Haghetti spoops
- Lire fighters
- Glubber roves

CHAPTER 2

> Sup a coup
> Poothtaste
> Palf a hound of Chensleydale wheeze
> and
> Baked beans
> (Gank thoodness)

During Writing

Invite students to write their own Lhopping Sist, I mean Shopping List. Students may prefer to work individually or in pairs. Encourage students to circle two or three 'items' from their lists that sound like great stories and develop one into a story title.

After Writing

Invite students to share two or three binomials from their lists that they believe are the most fantastic, including developed story titles. Also invite students who may have begun developing their story from their title to share some or all of that writing.

Sharing Student Writing

> Tairy fale
> Caredy scat   *The Amazing Adventures of Brave the Caredy Scat*
> Ficture prame   *The Ficture Prame of Life*
> Bote tag   *Bote Tag's Wonderful Day*
> Chidewalk salk
> Phell cone
> Boupon cook
> Wop statch
> Doset cloor   *Through the Doset Cloor*
> Loor flamp
> Bow snoots
> Daseball biamond   *Daseball Biamonds are a Girl's Best Friend*
> Power flot
>   -Melody

REFERENCE

Carter, J., & Denton, G. (2009). *Orange silver sausage: A collection of poems without rhymes*. London: Walker Books.

WHAT I WON'T AND WILL MISS

Nora Ephron's (2010) *I Remember Nothing: And Other Reflections* is a memoir, chockfull of humorous and witty stories about her life as a journalist and screenplay writer. At the back of the book she includes a list of What I Won't and Will Miss after she dies (p. 132). At the time this book was written, Ephron was living with Leukaemia. To me, this list is neither depressing nor macabre; rather, it invites thinking about what matters in life. I like to share this list with students because the invitation to think about what matters to a person creates meaningful, authentic opportunities for writing.

Before Writing

Begin a discussion on significant events in one's life. For young children such events may include going into a new grade, learning how to ride a bike, or turning 10 (the significance of a double digit age). For older students, topics of interest may include starting high school, adolescence, living with more than one parent, or perhaps recovering from personal illness. Encourage students to share some of their ideas, paying special attention to how these ideas can be thought of in terms of what will/ will not be missed e.g., what I won't miss about my dog / what I will miss about my dog. Finally, read Ephron's What I Won't and Will Miss list.

What I Won't Miss	*What I Will Miss*
Dry skin	My kids
Bad dinners like the one we went to last night	Nick
E-mail	Spring
Technology in general	Fall
My closet	Waffles
Washing my hair	The concept of waffles
Bras	Bacon
Funerals	A walk in the park
Illness everywhere	The idea of a walk in the park
Polls that show that 32 percent of the American people believe in creationism	The park
	Shakespeare in the Park
Polls	The bed
Fox TV	Reading in bed
The collapse of the dollar	Fireworks
Bar mitzvahs	Laughs
Mammograms	The view out the window
Dead flowers	Twinkle lights
The sound of the vacuum cleaner	Butter
Bills	Dinner at home just the two of us

CHAPTER 2

E-mail. I know I already said it, but I want to emphasize it.	Dinner with friends
Dinner with friends in cities where none of us lives
Small print	Paris
Panels on Women in Film	Next year in Istanbul
Taking off makeup every night	Pride and Prejudice
	The Christmas tree
	Thanksgiving dinner
	One for the table
	The dogwood
	Taking a bath
	Coming over the bridge to Manhattan
	Pie

During Writing

Invite students to write their own list of What I Won't And Will Miss. The tone and subject matter of students' lists can and should vary, from light-hearted (e.g., what I won't/will miss about Grade Three), to heartfelt (e.g., what I won't/will miss about my friend moving away), to serious (e.g., what I won't/will miss about being sick). Encourage students to circle one or two ideas from their lists that hold great story potential.

After Writing

Invite students to share the topic or theme of their list before reading a few lines.

Sharing Student Writing

What I Won't Miss	*What I Will Miss (about College)*
Gen Ed courses	Meaningful Gen Ed courses
Campus jobs	The people you meet at campus jobs
Endless schoolwork	Schoolwork you learn from
Frat house parties	The entertainment at parties
Professors who don't notice you	Professors who influence and inspire
All-nighters	Bonding with sleep deprived friends
Friends with benefits	Friends with benefits that teach you about yourself
The Meal plan	Having the metabolism and low HDL to handle cheap food
Watered down booze	$1 pitchers of beer

Divas	Authentic people you meet
	-Bridget

What I Won't Miss	*What I Will Miss (about Studying Abroad in France)*
Windows without screens	Pain au chocolat. Daily.
Co-ed bathrooms	Getting caught in the rain in such gorgeous settings
Disgusting bars	Wine. All of the wine and the respect for wine
Disgusting men at disgusting bars	Cafés
Luggage and the TGV	le café. Real coffee.
The loneliness	That feeling of I-can-accomplish-anything-or-be-anyone
Feeling academically inadequate	Feeling revitalized, experiences expanding my mind
Heartache from missing my family	Independence
Being away from the theatre at home	My host family, la famille Dromard
Not having a confidante	Taking risks and feeling brave
-DePorre	

REFERENCE

Ephron, N. (2010). *I remember nothing: And other reflections.* New York, NY: Vintage.

CHAPTER 3

AESTHETIC GIFTS

BRING ME MAGIC

Susan Wooldridge's (1996) *Poemcrazy: Freeing Your Life with Words* is a collection of writing invitations designed to inspire and motivate people to write poetry. The poem, "Bring Me Magic" (p. 109) invites students to self-select meaningful or simply unique objects and to write about them in a three-line poem. I like to share this poem with students because the form is simple yet powerful. In the words of Fletcher (2002), it is "short and potent" (p. 13). Writing about found objects also teaches students the power of observation, to notice details and to use them to develop ideas in writing.

Before Writing

Begin a discussion with students on objects they cherish. What qualities do they like about them? Next, pass around a basket of found, aesthetic objects (e.g., sea shells, dried flowers, rocks, smooth stones, twigs, etc.) and ask students to pick just one. For those who ask, "Which one should I pick? Simply tell them to choose an object that intrigues them in some way. After they have selected an object, tell students to take a minute and study it (e.g., turn the object over, observe its shape, texture, size, and colour etc.). Read "Bring Me Magic" to students, a poem written by a student in Grade 7 whose found object was a dried flower.

> Dead rose
> Crinkly as paper
> Bring me love

During Writing

Invite students to write their own Bring Me Magic poem using the object they picked from the basket. First, ask students to name their object. The name can be real or made up. Next, ask students to describe it (e.g., what does it look like?) and compare it to something else. Comparisons may use *like* or *as* or *is* (e.g., love is a red, red, rose). In the third and final line, students ask the object to bring a quality they need (e.g., bring me happiness; bring me health; bring me peace, etc.).

CHAPTER 3

After Writing

Invite individual students to share what they have written. Because these poems are short, encourage several students to share their poems. If the writing is figurative or abstract (i.e. does not reveal what the object is), students may enjoy reading their poems without showing their found object and asking the class to share what they think their poem is about.

Sharing Student Writing

Heated mattress pad	Sound of the ocean	Victor Pinecone
Thick as a fallow field	Pure as joy	Crackly as a snowflake
Bring me sleep	Bring me home	Bring me new life
-Sheila	-DePorre	-Andrew

Weathered walnut	Elijah Bell	Firecracker flower
Rough as gravel	Beauty, unheard	Bursting bright, booming light
Bring me squirrels	Bring me ears	Bring me the 4th of July
-Heather	-Megan	-Laurie

Littlest Traveller
Tiny as a penny
Bring me the ocean
 -Natasha

REFERENCES

Fletcher, R. (2002). *Poetry matters: Writing a poem from the inside out.* New York, NY: HarperCollins.
Wooldridge, S. (1996). *Poemcrazy: Freeing your life with words.* New York, NY: Three Rivers Press.

AESTHETIC GIFTS

POKING A HOLE

I came across this drawing/writing engagement from perusing a book at a National Art Educators Association (NAEA) conference years ago. I did not buy that book nor did I write down the title so I cannot provide a reference. Still, I like to share "Poking a Hole" with students because it combines drawing and writing. In particular, it invites students to attend to visual details from their quick-draws to help write a descriptive sentence.

Before Writing

Begin a discussion with students on objects with holes. At first, initial responses will be obvious (e.g., Swiss cheese, doughnuts, etc.) but once these are mentioned and out of the way students will be able to contribute more complex responses (e.g., fabric, cork board, foam, etc.).

During Writing

Invite students to create their own story by Poking A Hole. Ask students to lift a page, any page, from their notebooks and poke or strike a random hole in the page with a sharp pencil. Tell students not to worry about the hole being pretty or perfect. Next, tell students to write around the hole as many words (i.e. nouns) as they can think of that have holes. Once students have a list of ten or more words, tell them to choose one word, turn the page over, and do a quick-draw of that word, incorporating the poked hole in the drawing (e.g., drawing a slice of Swiss cheese around the hole). Remind students that quick-draws have nothing to do with drawing ability; rather, they are about constructing meaning visually. Write two or three sentences about that word.

After Writing

Invite students to show their quick-sketch on a document scanner or overhead projector while they read what they have written. Some students may prefer to only read their writing; however, encourage students to show their quick-sketches while they read their writing since both sign systems or communication systems support each other.

Sharing Student Writing

Inner tube	Donut	Bagel
Swiss cheese	Pineapple ring	Nose
Worm-eaten leaf	Worn socks	Key loop
Wooly sweater	Aged underwear	
-Sarah		

CHAPTER 3

Cup	Acoustic guitar (*)	Black hole
Note	Old books	Well
Bottle caps	Garbage cans	Protractor

An acoustic guitar has a hole. It is a six-stringed instrument.
    -Vamsi, Grade 5

NEWSPAPER BLACKOUT

Austin Kleon's (2010) *Newspaper Blackout* is a book of redacted poems from different sections of the newspaper. Poems about love, family, and friendship emerge from unlikely pages such as the finance and business sections. Writer, cartoonist, and designer, Kleon inspires people to pick up black felt tipped pens and begin their own blackout poems from newspapers. I like to share selected examples of blackout poems with students because the redacted text illuminates unique word combinations and potential story ideas.

Before Writing

Begin a discussion with students on discovering stories within stories. Project any newspaper page on a document camera or overhead projector so that everyone can see the page. Next, circle or box a particular word that stands out and then circle other words (e.g., nouns, verbs, adjectives, etc.) that you think might make sense with that first circled word. Try not to force a story. Just let words speak to you. Once several words have been circled, quickly redact the remaining text. Read these words aloud and redact any unnecessary words. Next, talk about how the remaining words tell a story. Finally, read the following three blackout poems from the book and discuss what stories they tell.

Children	I prove	A Mother's
play	to	Forgiveness
to keep sane	be	is A sigh
(p. 30)	a	and
	Major	a
	ladies'	Clean Up
	man	After an extended silence
	when he	in
	lets	a seat near the
	me	wall
	borrow the car	(p. 59)
	(p. 45)	

During Writing

Invite students to create their own Newspaper Blackout poem. Distribute various sections of a newspaper (e.g., sports, business, finance, travel) to individual or pairs of students. Tell students to circle or box words that stand out to them throughout their piece. Students may locate what Kleon calls an anchor word (e.g., 'church') that sets the tone for the piece (e.g., poem about religion) and impacts other circled word choices (e.g., look for spiritual words). Students may prefer to let a poem emerge without trying to control or direct it. Once students feel they have enough words to tell a story, remind them to cover up remaining text with chisel tipped markers so that only the words they circled stand out. This is called redacting. If some words are far apart, they can resolve this by creating what Kleon calls 'rivers' where students draw a line to connect two words. Kleon typically uses the white space between words and sentences to create "clean rivers" among words. Rivers can be helpful because they tell you in what order to read words.

After Writing

Invite students to share their blackout poems. Students may read them from their seats or project them on the Elmo so that others can experience the poem visually while they read. Blackout poems tumble down the page and offer a unique visual experience.

Sharing Student Writing

> the sun
> is
> damasked
> in
> delight
> that
> treads
> by Heaven
>   -April

REFERENCE

Kleon, A. (2010). *Newspaper blackout*. New York, NY: Harper.

WATERCOLOUR CUBES

Ken Nordine's (2000) *Colors* and O'Neil's (1990) *Hailstones and Halibut Bones: Adventures in Poetry and Color* provide a collection of poems on colour. Colours are unique (e.g., olive and burgundy, chartreuse and indigo), some of which have personalities (e.g., Lavender is an old old old old lady). I like to share these books with students because they inspired what I call "Watercolour Cubes" which combine painting and writing. Specifically, students attend to hue and shade from their cubes that help generate descriptive words, which can be used to craft a sentence or improve an existing story title.

Before Writing

Begin a discussion with students about colour. Which colour(s) do you like? What kind of feelings do you associate with particular colours? Next, colour a small square with a watercolour pencil on watercolour paper. Colour over the square with a complementary colour (e.g., yellow over orange) or the same colour but with a different intensity (e.g., yellow ochre over lemon yellow). Cut and glue the cube to the writer's notebook and project on a document camera so that everyone can see the colour cube. Next, spit on your thumb or forefinger and make small concentric circles over the watercolour cube to loosen the pigment. Students generally like to do this though some teachers may prefer to use a damp paintbrush or the corner of a damp cloth. Write as many word associations as you can think of that remind you of that colour. These associations can be a variety of sounds, smells, feelings, or objects. The first few associations will be obvious (e.g., dark brown, light blue) but, with further brainstorming, word associations become more specific (e.g., sienna, ecru, scarlet, etc.). Push for the specific; it supports vivid writing. Finally, read Nordine's (2000) "Lavender is" and/or O'Neill's (1990) "What is Brown?" and invite students to share which lines stand out to them and discuss why.

Lavender is an old old old old lady	Brown is the colour of a country road
lavender is	Back of a turtle
aren't you?	Back of a toad.
I thought you were lady lavender in	
the indigo house	Brown is cinnamon
by the purple wood	And morning toast
cobwebbed spiders and magic magenta	And the good smell of
lavender	
keeper of dark corners	The Sunday roast.
and black blue blood	Brown is the colour of work
lady of the soft edges	And the sound of a river,
tell us all	Brown is bronze and a bow
or tell me	And a quiver.

CHAPTER 3

> where day goes with night
> and what they do there
> and what it means
> the questions fall on your lavender lap
> and your answer is
> a lavender laugh in a lavender cry
> near a lavender what by a lavender why

> Brown is the house
> On the edge of town
> Where wind is tearing
> The shingles down.
> Brown is a freckle
> Brown is a mole
> Brown is the earth
> When you dig a hole.
> Brown is the hair
> On many a head
> Brown is chocolate
> And gingerbread.
> Brown is a feeling
> You get inside
> When wondering makes
> Your mind grow wide.
> Brown is a leather shoe
> And a good glove
> Brown is as comfortable
> As love.

During Writing

Invite students to create their own Watercolour Cube using the same steps as modelled. To save time, create watercolour cubes in advance and randomly distribute to students. Remind students to keep their pens, pencils, and gel pens moving in a quick-write. In Watercolour Cubes, initial words may be basic (e.g., green) but it is important to get those generic words out of the way to make room for more specific, vivid ones (e.g., glistening bruise green).

After Writing

Invite students to share a few colour descriptions and their descriptive sentence. Time permitting, the teacher may invite students to do a line-around where students take turns around the room (in a popcorn fashion, not round robin) and read their descriptive sentence using one or more of their colour words.

Sharing Student Writing

| Peppered mac-n-cheese | Late fall gourd | Jack-o-lantern mush |
| Butternut squash | Crushed orange leaves | Sunspot |

Rotten orange (*)	Tangerine, squashed	Orange, dirty
Ginger hair	Pus	Alley tabby cat
Decaying carrot (*)	Barbeque potato chips	Fake tan orange

My grandmother's sweater with its shades of decaying carrot, smelled like rotten root.

    -Nate

Grass	Wrapping paper	Hosta
Roses	Springtime	Grasshopper
Jalapeño (*)	Salad	Watercress

Her eyes were jalapeño green and full of spice.

    -Sarah

Orange (*)	Sunset	Fire
Comets (*)	Meteors	Light
Star		

The sky was bright, a comet orange.

    -Vamsi, Grade 5

REFERENCES

Nordine, K. (2000). *Colors*. New York, NY: Harcourt.

O'Neil, M. (1990). *Hailstones and halibut bones: Adventures in poetry and color*. New York, NY: Doubleday Books.

CHAPTER 3

VIBRANT DYE

Iris McClellan Tiedt's (2002) *Tiger Lilies, Toadstools, and Thunderbolts: Engaging K-8 Students with Poetry* is a resource book on creative approaches to teaching and experiencing poetry. I like to share a particular image from this book with students (p. 160) because it inspired "Vibrant Dye" which combines food colouring and haiku, a Japanese form of poetry. Food colouring is just as good as paint, accessible, inexpensive, and does not stain. Tiedt suggests that students "present their original verses artistically" (p. 159), where the image-making may come after the writing. In Vibrant Dye, students rely instead on the serendipity of the movement of colour to promote written ideas.

Before Writing

Begin a discussion with students about colour and shape. What significance do particular colours and shapes hold for us? How can colour and shape corroborate what we feel? What connections can we experience between how we view images and our emotions to them? (For further reading on this topic, see Bang, 2000). Next, project Tiedt's untitled image on a document camera so that everyone can see how the spider-like image inspired a haiku on winter and trees. Even though this image is black and white, talk about how colour might affect our viewing of the image. Continue the conversation about the spindly lines and the feelings they conjure up. Invite a student to read the poem in class.

> Winter wind whistles;
> Rude, crude, arrogant pusher,
> Bow, gracious silk tree.

During Writing

Invite students to create their own Vibrant Dye image as a pathway toward descriptive writing. Cut a variety of shapes (e.g., triangles, squares, etc.) of watercolour grade paper or cardstock and distribute to students. Distribute bottles of food colouring (neon colours are ideal), straws, and paper plates as well. Ask students to place their paper on top of the plate to protect tables. Tell students to lightly mark all sides of their paper a, b, c, etc. with a pencil so that it can be eased later. Next, tell students to drop a few drops of colour onto their paper and, with their straws, blow close to the colour so that it moves along the page. As the colour dries, tell everyone to turn their vibrant dye image to the "A" position and ask, "What do you see?" Next, tell students to turn their image to the "B" position, and so forth. I find labelling the page helps students to consider all four sides. Whenever I do not ask students to label, many insist they do not see anything significant. In short, labelling offers focus. Once students can make a connection between what they see and how they feel about it, they are ready to write. Remind students that what they write is not a question of it being good or not; it has to be "good for the soul" (Fletcher, 2002, p. 14).

Haiku typically consists of 17 syllables written in three lines, 5, 7, and 5 respectively. Traditional poems are also connected to nature in some way. In Vibrant Dye, the haiku can be traditional or unconventional. Encourage students to make their own choice. Remind students that rich writing comes from within. Pay more attention to what you want to say rather than the form or structure through which you tell it.

After Writing

Invite individual students to share their images with their poems. Students may enjoy showing their vibrant dye images first, asking the class to share what they think their poem is about, and then read their poem. This approach invites discussion on the power of viewing and using language to capture our understanding of visual elements.

Sharing Student Writing

Dead Bug
Not in my house
Chills, screaming, disgusting
I saw him crawling up the wall
Whap! Splat!
    -Sarah

The forest sits still and untouched
No light enters
No light escapes
Branches, leafless
Darkness is King
Ruling the land of the unknown.
    -Saloni, Grade 7

Green forest
Pine leaves, needle sharp
Yellow flame, burning
Lifting
Floating
In a small space of white
Where are the firemen?
    -Joseph, Grade 11

REFERENCES

Bang, M. (2000). *Picture this: How pictures work.* San Francisco, CA: Seastar.
Fletcher, R. (2002). *Poetry matters: Writing a poem from the inside out.* New York, NY: HarperCollins.
Tiedt, I. M. (2002) *Tiger lilies, toadstools, and thunderbolts: Engaging K-8 students with poetry.* Newark, DL: International Reading Association.

CHAPTER 3

CLIP N CREATE

I have long been fascinated with the practice of cutting up writing, a technique popularized in the 1950s and 60s and often referred to as the cut up movement. I like to share "Clip N Create" with students because it is serendipitous (i.e. you never know what story idea you can create from a bag of cut-up words) and calls on students to think about how font, size, and colour affect tone and meaning of words (e.g., red letters for expressions of love or anger; large, bold letters for emphasis).

Before Writing

Begin a discussion with students on how font, size, and colour affect tone and meaning of words. Put a handful of cut-up words on a document camera and spread them out so that everyone can see them. Select a few words from the cluster and talk about their impact and why you might use one over the other. Begin to piece words together that either tell a story or simply communicate an idea. Challenge students to help you use only the words available or simplify the task by adding words by writing them in. Ask students to think about how the words magnify a person? A place? A mood? A voice? An idea? Finally, read student examples to students. Words in CAPS refer to those found in newspapers, magazines, etc.

During Writing

Invite students to create their own cut-up story or descriptive line by using Clip N Create word bags. Students may work independently, in pairs, or small groups. Distribute snack-size bags of pre-cut words from magazines, newspapers, flyers, etc. (Bags prepared in advance offer students more time to organize and construct ideas). If limited to words only in the bag, remind students that they can tear off letters to create words needed (e.g., "a" from "an"). To secure the cut-up creation, students may tape or glue words directly in their writer's notebooks.

After Writing

Invite students to share their clip n create creations. Because cut-up writing is usually short, encourage students to share more than one line. Encourage students to briefly share how the font, size, and/or colour of their words affect the tone and meaning of their sentence or poem.

Sharing Student Writing

EPIC SUPER powers are only in HOLLYWOOD and they are not FREE.
    -Joseph, Grade 11

Eat HEALTHY so you have energy for the next time you hit the ice. PROTECT the puck and take a hit to make a play. PAIN is temporary; pride is forever. And lastly, WIN.

    -Tyler, Grade 11

ENJOY THE SWEET things in life and you will FEEL BETTER. Do this and you can also never LOSE.

    -Sabrina, Grade 10

YOU lend the PAGES to my FABRIC.

    -Rachel

CHAPTER 3

BODY MAP

Jeff Kinney's (2008) "List Your Injuries" (p. 47) in *Diary of a Wimpy Kid Do-It-Yourself Book* inspired "Body Map" writing. I like to share this vacant list with students (i.e. vacant because Kinney wants writers to write their own) because it invites authentic discussion about their own injuries or injuries sustained by close friends or family members including pets. Body Map takes Kinney's idea one step further by combining quick-drawing with writing where students sketch a simple body outline of themselves (not to scale!) and mark with an X on their outline each place where they had an injury. I have yet to meet a writer who will not share a personal story of injury, quick-sketch and X their body, and then write about it.

Before Writing

Begin a discussion with students on injuries they have experienced. Some students may prefer to share stories that concern people they know like a family member or pet. Next, in the writer's notebook projected on a document camera, quickly sketch a generic outline of a body much like one sees at a crime scene. Mark an X at each location of the body where you experienced an injury. Injuries can be traumatic (e.g., required surgery) or common (e.g., scraped knee) or a combination of both. Some students like to distinguish significant injuries (X) from insignificant ones (x) with upper and lower case letters. Finally, choose one X that you think marks the spot for the greatest story potential and circle it. With the five senses in mind (i.e., sight, smell, sound, taste and touch), which help bring sensory details to the surface, write two or three sentences that describe what happened (e.g., "I can still remember the taste of metal in my mouth, blood trickling from the corner like a vampire").

During Writing

Invite students to create their own Body Map, a quick-draw outline of their bodies. Remind students that a generic outline is sufficient; however, some distinguishing characteristics are fine (e.g., a tall person may draw long legs). Mark the outline with as many X's as needed that identify where an injury occurred. Circle one X-injury that you want to write about. Write two or three sentences describing this injury. Remind students that using sensory details in their writing to develop ideas will help them to show, not tell, what happened.

After Writing

Invite a few students to share their body map and body map story. While students read their body map stories, some may enjoy projecting their body map outlines on the document scanner so that peers can see a visual history of personal injury.

Sharing Student Writing

I was about 5 or 6 and playing in the basement. Mom called me up for dinner. I walked to the stairs and smelled stir-fry. *I hated stir-fry.* I fell backwards, tumbled down the stairs, and cut my head on the stair. Eight stitches. No stir-fry.

-Sarah

One day I was at the beach and suddenly I felt a stinging pain in my leg. As soon as I felt it, I jumped out of the water. I swam to the shore and examined my knee. My mom came over and said it was nothing. *But I knew it wasn't nothing.* Later that night, I looked at my knee again and saw that I had been stung by a jelly fish. Not just once but at least five times. This was no ordinary jellyfish; its stings were much more powerful.

-Shelli, Grade 7

A couple of years ago I got a chin up bar from my uncle for my birthday. I put it up on my doorway and was doing a bunch of pull ups. One day I was getting tired, my hands sweaty. I went to do another pull up when snap! The bar came off the door in the middle of a pull up and sliced my chest open.

-Tyler, Grade 11

REFERENCE

Kinney, J. (2008). *Diary of a wimpy kid do-it-yourself book.* New York, NY: Amulet Books.

CHAPTER 3

FIX YOU

In 2005, the British rock band *Coldplay* released the song "Fix You." Lead singer Chris Martin apparently wrote the song for his wife, actress Gwyneth Paltrow, as a tribute to her late father Bruce Paltrow. I like to share this song with older students in particular because the notion of fixing oneself, something, or someone else is an idea I believe many can relate to in some meaningful way. Song lyrics are also jam-packed with emotion and imagery and take on a poetic form, a structure that invites students to explore their own.

Before Writing

Begin a discussion with the title of the song, Fix You. Ask, what do these words make you think about? What would you fix about yourself or someone else? Play the song Fix You and project the song lyrics on a document camera so students can follow the words while they listen. Continue the discussion about what the song means to everyone.

> When you try your best, but you don't succeed
> When you get what you want, but not what you need
> When you feel so tired, but you can't sleep
> Stuck in reverse
>
> And the tears come streaming down your face
> When you lose something you can't replace
> When you love someone, but it goes to waste
> Could it be worse?
>
> Lights will guide you home
> And ignite your bones
> And I will try to fix you
>
> And high up above or down below
> When you're too in love to let it go
> But if you never try you'll never know
> Just what you're worth
>
> Lights will guide you home
> And ignite your bones
> And I will try to fix you
>
> Tears stream down on your face
> When you lose something you cannot replace
> Tears stream down on your face

AESTHETIC GIFTS

And I...
Tears stream down on your face
I promise you I will learn from my mistakes
Tears stream down on your face
And I...

Lights will guide you home
And ignite your bones
And I will try to fix you

During Writing

Invite students to listen to the song and write their own lyrics to Fix You. Some students may prefer to listen to the song from their iPods or iPhones. To create a listening climate, dim the classroom lights (if possible) and encourage students to close their eyes or rest their heads on their desks so that they can focus entirely on the lyrics and melody. Where some students may prefer to write during the song others may wait until the song is done. With the song lyrics still projected, tell students that their writing may include some original song lyrics much like Olivia's piece below.

After Writing

Invite a few students to share their song lyrics. Another option is to invite students to share just one stanza that they feel best captures the essence of what their song is about.

Sharing Student Writing

> When you try your best, but you don't succeed
> *I didn't know why they kept hitting me, punching me, and kicking me, I tried to stop them but they hit me harder.*
> When you get what you want, but not what you need
> *They were all supposedly my friends. They were all I ever wanted because they treated me nice and accepted me for who I am, I thought.*
> When the tears come streaming down your face
> *I couldn't stop myself from crying as they punched me harder and blood spat out of my mouth.*
> When you lose something you can't replace
> *They stole my purse, which contained some of my most treasured items like the picture of my grandpa and me, money I'd been saving for a year, and all of my school books.*

91

CHAPTER 3

When you love someone, but it goes to waste
The part that upset me the most is that they boy I used to like was part of that group. I guess I had chosen the wrong person.
Lights will guide you home and ignite your bones
As soon as they stopped I hoped and prayed someone would come find me. I just kept following streetlights.
Tears stream down on your face; I promise you I will learn from my mistakes
It took me hours to crawl to my house.
Tears stream down on your face and I will try to fix you
When my mom opened the door and saw me almost unconscious, she screamed, picked me up, and immediately asked what happened and I explained it all.
I will try to fix you.
   -Olivia, Grade 7

When he fought so hard, but didn't succeed,
Your heart starts racing indeed.
When you feel so tired, but cannot sleep,
Your mind is off track
Your heart in strain
You think this can't be fact.
Tears come down your face.
This is someone you cannot replace.
Tracks of memories fill your heart.
Then you realise, this is just the start.
   -Lee, *on her father passing away*

REFERENCE

Coldplay (2005). *Fix You*. You Tube.

A CLOSING DOOR

Roger Rosenblatt's (2011) *Unless it Moves the Human Heart: The Craft and Art of Writing* details one semester in his college writing course. Included are snippets of student talk about the joys and challenges of narrative craft. "A Closing Door" invites students to think about how the clicking sound of a closing door connects to their own lives. I like to share this engagement with students because it invites them to think about the story potential from an everyday sound like the gentle or harsh closing of a door.

Before Writing

Open and close the classroom door. Do this a couple of times and watch students listen. Next, tell students to close their eyes as you open and close the door one last time. With their eyes still closed, ask them to think of a time in their lives where the clicking sound of a door felt poignant. With their eyes open or closed, read the examples in the book from college students:

> A gay man from South Africa, whose partner had walked out on him, focused on the sound of the lock as the door of their apartment closed. "He said we didn't click," he wrote. "But the door clicked" (p. 24).

> A young man from Chicago...wrote about the Sunday morning his father walked out on his family. After the door closed, he and his mother, brothers, and sisters all sat down to eat pancakes. "Blueberry," he wrote. "They were blueberry" (p. 24).

> A woman in her forties, a marine scientist who lived on Cape Cod...wrote of growing up in trailers on navy bases. She began her essay, "In my father's house there were no doors" (p. 24).

During Writing

Invite students to write their own narrative of A Closing Door where they can capture, in just a few sentences, what that familiar click sound of a closed door means to them. Other possible variations include the sound of an opening door, someone banging on a door, sounds associated with hiding behind a door, muffled sounds heard from under a door, paws scraping under a door, etc.

After Writing

In a line-around, invite students to share one line from their writing until everyone in the room who wants to share has had an opportunity to do so. For students unsure of sharing, they can say, "Pass" until the next person shares.

CHAPTER 3

Sharing Student Writing

I sit alone in my room	The clicking-sound of a door lock closing. A door creaking open.
Quiet. Quiet. Quiet.	These sounds I've heard before. From horror movies.
Bzzzzzzzzz... *Click.*	They make the hair on the back of my neck stand up.
Someone is home,	They scare the crap out of me.
says the garage.	Late at night…
I think.	when I hear my brother shut the door…
I hope.	and it clicks loudly…
-Christine	I still get a little freaked out.
	It's like, *"Who's there?"*
	-Sean

REFERENCE

Rosenblatt, R. (2011). *Unless it moves the human heart: The craft and art of writing.* New York, NY: HarperCollins.

AESTHETIC GIFTS

ARE YOU LISTENING?

Debra Kuzbik's (1996) *Ready, Set, Write!: Creative Ideas to Get Kids Writing* offers teachers one hundred writing activities for their students. Writing activity #61, "Are you Listening?" invites students to listen to a read aloud of Byrd Baylor's (1997) *The Other Way to Listen* and consider what sounds they can assign to natural objects (e.g., seed, rock, and pine cone). I like to share this book with students because it invites them to think about sound from unlikely places and write unique ways to describe what they 'hear.'

Before Writing

Begin a discussion with students on onomatopoeia, a literary term that means the imitation of sound. Many animal sounds, for example, are onomatopoeic such as rabbits that *squeak* or horses that *neigh*. Younger students may recognize a lot of onomatopoeia in Dr. Seuss books such as the 1970 classic *Mr. Brown Can Moo! Can you?* Using a few found objects, I want students to think about possible sounds any one of these objects may make. I ask Kuzbik's questions, does the object sing or murmur? Does it speak or laugh? What does it say to you? (p. 58). To demonstrate listening, I can do one of several things. I can wrap my hands around the object to get a sense of what sound it makes; I can put the object up to my ear (e.g., conch shell); I can blow air on it; I can close my eyes and imagine this object in its natural environment or habitat and the sounds I would expect to hear (e.g., Gale winds wrapping around my shell).

During Writing

Scatter small, natural items such as seeds, nuts, pinecones, leaves, rocks, petals or seashells. Invite students to choose one object from the table they are interested in writing about. Ask students to take a moment to listen to their object. Next, invite students to write their own narrative of Are You Listening, where they freely write whatever message their object conveys to them. Remind students to focus on sound.

After Writing

Invite several students to share their writing. Students may hold out their object while they read or pass it around so that others can feel its texture.

Sharing Student Writing

> You open softly like a cloud, softer than the sound of butterfly wings.
> I hear you.

CHAPTER 3

>You whisper of sweet perfume.
>In the breeze, I hear you.
>Morning dew collects on your lips.
>Your story is short yet powerful.
>You bear fruit that will grow into another.
>You speak the language of the Earth. I hear your voice.
>>-Alison, *whose found object is a flower*

REFERENCES

Baylor, B. (1997). *The other way to listen.* New York, NY: Aladdin.
Kuzbik, D. (1996). *Ready, set, write!: Creative ideas to get kids writing.* Winnipeg: Peguis.
Seuss. D. (1970). *Mr. Brown can moo! Can you?* New York, NY: Random House.

CHAPTER 4

WORD CRAFT

FAT, MUSCLE, & CHOLESTEROL

Long ago, I stumbled across the line, "Adjectives are fat; verbs are muscles (adverbs are cholesterol) by J. Patrick Lewis, winner of the National Council of Teachers of English 2011 Excellence in Children's Poetry Award. American poet John Frederick Nims before him also described verbs as muscle. For Nims, nouns are bones and adverbs, not just adjectives, are fat. I like to share Lewis' quote with students because the words fat, muscle, and cholesterol can refer to any number of ideas, making the invitation to write open but also a place to write about a topic in which one may feel expert or knowledgeable.

Before Writing

Begin a discussion with students on topics of interest. This pool of ideas should be broad (e.g., art) so that specifics can be considered from broad topics (e.g., impressionism, cubism, Harlem Renaissance). As students popcorn their ideas aloud, the teacher can write them down as a list of shared ideas that students may refer to later. Finally, read Lewis' quote which concerns the topic of writing. Discuss what this line tells readers about what matters to Lewis as a writer.

Adjectives are fact; verbs are muscles (adverbs are cholesterol)

During Writing

Invite students to write their own Fat, Muscle, & Cholesterol. First, ask students to think about a topic that interests them. Next, ask students to consider what is important about their topic (i.e. the fat of their idea), essential (i.e. the muscle of their idea), and least important (i.e. the cholesterol of their idea) and write their quote using Lewis' structure with the semi colon and parentheses.

After Writing

Invite individual students to share what they have written. Because these quotes are brief, encourage several students to share their writing. To feel the full weight of someone's position on a topic, students may enjoy rearranging words for effect; Example:

CHAPTER 4

Algebra is fat; trigonometry is muscle (geometry is cholesterol)
Geometry is fat; algebra is muscle (trigonometry is cholesterol)

Sharing Student Writing

    Freedom is fat; choice is muscle (structure is cholesterol)
    Outliers are fat; correlations are muscle (biases are cholesterol)
    Facts are fat; primary documents are muscles (textbooks are cholesterol)
    Names of historical figures are fat; a broader understanding of an event/period is muscle (dates are cholesterol)
    Notes are fat; thinking and problem solving are muscle (worksheets are cholesterol)
        -Anonymous

    Blush is fat; mascara is muscle (concealer is cholesterol)
        -Danielle

ALTER A CLICHÉ

Art Peterson's (1996) *The Writer's Workout Book: 113 Stretches Toward Better Prose* offers a collection of writing ideas through several themed chapters. "Alter a Cliché" (p. 228) invites students to craft an original idea by revising a cliché. A cliché is a worn out expression or idea. If overused, a cliché can really lose its effect. I like to share a few altered clichés from Peterson's list with students because it invites them to think about the idea potential from a worn out expression by tweaking it, making it their own, and ultimately giving their story an effect.

Before Writing

Begin a discussion with students on clichés. Extend the discussion to include idioms, which are sometimes confused with clichés. An idiom, a figurative expression where meaning is implied, can be a cliché but a cliché is not always an idiom. Read some examples of clichés to get the conversation going about which ones students use in free discourse. Some examples include:

One foot in the grave; When all is said and done; Burn the candle at both ends; Grin and bear it; Live and let live; Look for a needle in a haystack; Put all your eggs in one basket; Cry over spilt milk (p. 228). Finally, read the following altered clichés and discuss what makes them fresh or unique.

Time wounds all heels - Groucho Marx
Where there's a will there's a lawsuit - Addison Mizzen
There's been a lot of Perrier under the bridge since 1968 – Linda Ellerbee

During Writing

Invite students to write their own Alter A Cliché. Some students may prefer altering clichés they use frequently because they are more familiar. Other students may enjoy the challenge of trying to alter clichés that are somewhat new to them.

After Writing

Once students have finished writing, invite them to share their altered clichés one per person or, if students are sitting in groups, one person from each group may share his/her writing.

Sharing Student Writing

Selling like hot cakes; Selling like iPhones.
      -Julie

CHAPTER 4

It's raining cats and dogs; It's raining balloons and bubbles.
      -Sarah

REFERENCE

Peterson, A. (1996). *The writer's workout book: 113 stretches toward better prose.* Berkeley, CA: National Writing Project.

TRY TEN

Aimee Buckner's (2005) "Try Ten" (p. 62) in *Notebook Know How: Strategies for the Writer's Notebook* is a revision strategy for reworking leads, transition sentences, endings, etc. Try Ten involves rewriting a sentence ten different ways as an exercise for figuring out which sentence is most effective. I like to share this list with students because it invites them to think about how to express an idea more than one way. In writing their own try ten, students can use these sentences to locate a potential story title, revise an existing story title, find direction in the story they are writing, explore a new story idea, or discover a unique lead sentence to their story.

Before Writing

Begin a discussion with students about stories they have either written that have little or no focus as well as stories they want to write but feel unsure about how to get started. Encourage students to share what are the central themes or main ideas of their stories. Next, read fourth grade student Davis' list about country singer and songwriter Toby Keith. Discuss how Davis uses Try Ten to say Keith is a patriot without actually saying he is a patriot (p. 63). Each line offers something different, such as tone and story direction, about Toby Keith:

> Toby Keith is my hero because he loves our country more than anybody.
> Toby Keith fights for our country like President Bush and Dick Chaney put together.
> Toby Keith would make a better president than John Kerry.
> Watch out John Kerry, here comes Toby.
> Toby Keith is the greatest hero because he doesn't let anyone mess with America.
> I think people should like America as much as Toby Keith.
> Toby Keith stands for our country like a bulldozer.
> If you don't love America, Toby will make you think twice.
> Toby Keith is my everyday hero because he stands for our country like a rock.
> Go Toby!

During Writing

Invite students to write their own Try Ten, working from an existing story or a story idea not yet developed. Some students may prefer peer support to help generate the first five ideas.

After Writing

Invite students to self-select one line that either best captures what their story is about or is a good example of written craft.

CHAPTER 4

Sharing Student Writing

1. Time waits for no man.
2. Time is a limited resource for everyone.
3. You cannot recover Wasted Time.
4. Only the Universe can redeem stolen time that the locust has eaten up.
5. There is a season and a time for every purpose.
6. Time drags when you're young. After 30, time races to the finish line.
7. "You may delay but time does not." Wise words, Benjamin Franklin; wise words.
8. Time cannot be harnessed, collected, or dictated to by mankind no matter how much we progress as a species.
9. The final countdown; it belongs to time.

    -Sheila

1. My grandpa is the perfect role model.
2. Everyone loves my grandpa.
3. My grandpa is unbelievably kind.
4. My grandpas is the most generous man I know.
5. My grandpa is always there for me, no matter the circumstance.
6. My grandpa goes to church everyday.
7. My grandpa is 85 years old and still works out.
8. My grandpa is the most positive person I know.
9. My grandpa is not ashamed to say, "I love you," to me.
10. I would take a bullet for my grandpa.

    -Spencer

1. Cancer is The Night Thief stealing your health.
2. Cancer can make a good life go bad.
3. Cancer doesn't discriminate; it simply doesn't care.
4. Cancer doesn't have a right to live in people's bodies.
5. Cancer is the Unwelcome Guest.
6. Cancer makes you feel weak and unable.
7. Cancer makes you feel hopeless, sometimes.
8. Cancer causes pain to the body and shatters the soul.
9. Too often, cancer wins the battle of life.
10. Cancer can be A Second Chance on life.

    -Jacqueline

REFERENCE

Buckner, A. (2005). *Notebook know how: Strategies for the writer's notebook.* Portland, MN: Stenhouse.

NUMBERS INTO IMAGES

Art Peterson's (1996) *The Writer's Workout Book: 113 Stretches Toward Better Prose* offers a collection of writing ideas through several themed chapters. In "Numbers into Images" (p. 115), writers use language to express ideas in numbers. I like to share Isadora Alman's sentence with students in which she compares unemployment to a country-sized bowl of guacamole because writing about issues this way helps students not just visualize ideas that can sometimes get lost in numbers but also because it is a sophisticated way to express knowing.

Before Writing

Begin a discussion with students about current, relevant topics in the media. This may include headlines from newspapers in which numbers are expressed (.e.g., homelessness in the area; number of goals scored by the Toronto Maple Leafs). Read a few and talk about what they mean and how else they could be described or compared without using numbers. Finally, read the following number-into-image sentence by Isadora Alman.

If all the unemployed people in the US were avocados, they would make a guacamole the size of Guam (p. 115).

During Writing

Invite students to write their own Numbers Into Images. For some students, it may be worthwhile to leaf through newspapers or magazines for inspiration to write a number-into-image sentence. Other students may prefer to write about topics that are personal (e.g., drunk driving; bullying; relationships; sexuality).

After Writing

Invite students to share their number-into-image sentence. Encourage everyone to share.

Sharing Student Writing

If you compared the amount of estrogen to testosterone in teaching you would be comparing flocks of geese to sparrows.
 -Brian

If the US debt were water drops, we'd be underwater.
 -Caporale

REFERENCE

Peterson, A. (1996). *The writer's workout book: 113 stretches toward better prose.* Berkeley, CA: National Writing Project.

CHAPTER 4

ABSOLUTES

Harry Noden's (2011) *Image Grammar: Using Grammatical Structures to Teach Writing* is a practical book on writing that offers ways to 'paint' ideas with words through brushstroke lessons. In this book an absolute is one such way, a two-word combination of a noun and a –ing or –ed participle. I like to share absolutes with students because they strengthen writing by developing action in a sentence.

Before Writing

Begin a discussion with students on nouns (i.e. a person, place, or thing) and participles (words formed from verbs but used as adjectives). Tell students to close their eyes, just as Noden suggests, and "picture a mountain climber moving along a steep cliff" (p. 6). With this image in mind read the sentence, "The mountain climber edged along the cliff." With their eyes still closed, tell students that you are going to strengthen this mental picture by revising the sentence with absolutes. Next, read the line, "The mountain climber edged along the cliff, *hands shaking, feet trembling,*" and/or the same line in reverse, "*Hands shaking, feet trembling*, the mountain climber edged along the cliff" (p. 6). Tell students to open their eyes and discuss the differences between the sentence without the absolute and the ones with the absolutes.

During Writing

Invite students to write sentences using Absolutes. They may use both –ing and –ed participles or just one of their choosing. Some students may find it easier, at first, to write a sentence they would normally write and then revise their sentence by trying to develop their idea with an absolute. Remind students that three or more absolutes diminish the effect; one or two are best.

After Writing

Invite students to share their absolute sentences. If students have written multiple sentences, tell them to select the line they believe is a good example of craft in writing.

Sharing Student Writing

With your heart racing and knuckles tightening, you throw the first punch, a real knockout.
    -Joseph, Grade 11

Eyes rolling, stomach turning, I ate my dinner anyways.

I went on the roller coaster, heart racing, hair raising.
>-Jillian, Grade 7

Heart pounding, I stood up, picked up my violin and started feeling warm as if I were a pot of soup resting on a warm stove.
>-Helen, Grade 3

Sweat-dripping, legs-thr-thr-thr-thr-obbing, man my workout is tough this week.
>-Sean

REFERENCE

Noden, H. (1999). *Image grammar: Using grammatical structures to teach writing.* Portsmouth, NH: Heinemann.

CHAPTER 4

APPOSITIVES

Harry Noden's (2011) *Image Grammar: Using Grammatical Structures to Teach Writing* is a practical book on writing that offers ways to 'paint' ideas with words through brushstroke lessons. In this book an appositive is one such way, a noun that adds a second image to the preceding noun. I like to share appositives with students because they expand and enhance detail as well as clarify an idea for students who may only know one of the nouns, which is sometimes the case for dual language learners.

Before Writing

Begin a discussion with students on nouns they know to which they can assign a second image. I like to share my line, "I love to paint with *an old brush, a vintage*" to get them started. I also like to share some examples from eighth grade students in Noden's book: waterfalls, tilted pitchers; old woman, withered lady; and fish; slimy mass of flesh. Next, I read one of Noden's lines about raccoons and ask students to listen to how the author expands the appositive to an appositive phrase. Then I omit the appositive altogether from Noden's writing to help students see the effect of the brushstroke where the line now merely tells rather than shows.

> The raccoon, *a scavenger*, enjoys eating turtle eggs.
> The raccoon, *a midnight scavenger who roams lake shorelines in search of food*, enjoys eating turtle eggs. (p. 8)
> The raccoon enjoys eating turtle eggs.

During Writing

Invite students to write sentences using Appositives. They may write one or more, depending on time and their ease with the brushstroke. Just as with the absolute, some students may find it easier to write a sentence they would normally write (see example 3) and then revise their sentence by developing their idea with an appositive.

After Writing

Invite students to share their appositive sentences, including their original sentence if they wrote one.

Sharing Student Writing

The church, a place of worship, was filled with song.
> -Sarah

My heart skipped as a girl in a witch costume with glowing stars waved her wand, her special bow.

    -Helen, Grade 3

Looking at the big sign, a billboard longer than my grandmother's trailer, I got an idea. My master told me to never play around with a samurai, a sword to be taken only seriously.

    -Sean

REFERENCE

Noden, H. (1999). *Image grammar: Using grammatical structures to teach writing.* Portsmouth, NH: Heinemann.

CHAPTER 4

TRANSFORMING A SENTENCE

Darren Crovitz's (2011) "Transforming a Sentence" from his article "Sudden Possibilities: Porpoises, Eggcorns, and Error" is one of ten language exercises that invites students to recast a sentence by making it appropriate to other contexts. I like to share Crovitz's transformations of the theme, "You're Fired" (p. 37) with students because it invites them to think about tone in writing. Taking Crovitz's idea one step further, I offer students the leads *formal talk, friendly talk,* and *street talk* which establish a direction to facilitate their own transformations.

Before Writing

Begin a discussion on tone, how someone feels about a given topic or subject. What kind of words do we use when we feel rash or courteous? How do these words change when we talk to friends, teachers, or colleagues? To keep the conversation going, offer the sentence starter "You're fired," and in a whole group discussion talk about the different ways to tell someone he has lost his job. Remind students that in formal talk, the language is sophisticated; in friendly talk the language is relaxed but respectful; in street talk the language is very casual which may include mainstream terms or phrases or even neologisms or made up words. As students provide examples, categorize them as examples of formal, friendly, or street talk. Finally, read Crovitz's transformations of "You're fired".

> We regret to inform you that your professional services are no longer required.
> Sorry, Bob, but with the poor economy we have to let you go.
> Get out now and don't come back!

During Writing

Invite students to write their own Transforming A Sentence, by transforming the themes, "I love you" and "Dining out" in formal, friendly, and street talk. Remind students that their word choice will let readers know whom they are addressing.

After Writing

Invite students to share one or all three sentences transformations. Peers may enjoy identifying which lines they think are examples of formal, friendly, and street talk.

Sharing Student Writing

> I care deeply for you. I love you.   Babe, you mean the world to me.
> Love you, honey.   Love ya, no matter what.

You're my favourite.　　　　　Yo, my heart be pumpin' for you *girllll*.
　　-Sarah　　　　　　　　　　-Nina

The pheromones that you emit have caused a chemical reaction in my body that implies compatibility.
I love you and the way you've helped me be a better person.
You're my boo.
　　　　-Dave

Nice to see you.
Hi!
What's up?
　　　　-Cerise, Grade 6

REFERENCE

Crovitz, D. (2011). Sudden possibilities: Porpoises, eggcorns, and error. *English Journal, 100*(4), 31–38.

CHAPTER 4

ADJECTIVES SHIFTED

Harry Noden's (2011) *Image Grammar: Using Grammatical Structures to Teach Writing* is a practical book on writing that offers ways to 'paint' ideas with words through brushstroke lessons. Noden's adjectives-shifted-out-of-order, or what I call simply "Adjectives Shifted" involves leaving one adjective in its place and shifting two others around it. I like to share Adjectives Shifted with students because this brushstroke magnifies an image, a particularly helpful lesson for those who tend to cluster several adjectives together (e.g., Penny is a beautiful, friendly, black poodle) or what Noden calls a "three-in-a-row string" (p. 9).

Before Writing

Begin a discussion on three-in-a-row string sentences. Ask students to close their eyes and listen to the sentence, "The large, red-eyed, angry bull moose charged the intruder" (p. 9). Ask students, what do you notice? What do you hear? Most importantly, what do you remember? Unsurprisingly, we rarely remember details when sentences are overloaded with too many descriptions. With their eyes still closed, read the same sentence where Noden shifts the adjectives to amplify details about the moose: "The large bull moose, red-eyed and angry, charged the intruder." Tell students to open their eyes and discuss the differences between the two sentences.

During Writing

Invite students to write sentences using Adjectives Shifted. Some students may find it easier to first write a sentence with three consecutive adjectives and then shift them.

After Writing

Invite students to share their writing. For especially reluctant writers, they may prefer to share only the adjectives they shifted.

Sharing Student Writing

> A small child, lonely and afraid, lay in the sterile hospital bed.
> -Sarah

> The adorable puppy, clumsy and snuggly, fell into my arms.
> -Ashley

The smelly raccoon, dark and rabid, nestled through the trashcans.
 -Sean

REFERENCE

Noden, H. (2011). *Image grammar: Using grammatical structures to teach writing.* Portsmouth, NH: Heinemann.

THE WRITING PROMISE[1]

I, _____ promise to write. I promise to write wherever paper (or napkins, wrapping paper, receipts, scrap paper), or a computer is at hand. I promise to remember that in whatever medium I chose for writing, there is no requirement to write every day. I do promise, however, to write whenever I can because I know that only through meaningful practice can the notebook or computer become a wellspring of ideas that really matter to me. When given a choice, I promise to write a card rather than send an electronic one.

I promise to read as a way of learning about author's craft. I promise to practice any written craft that strikes me and not scold myself later for writing in the style of someone else. Imitation, I must remember, is not stealing. I promise to stay open to all genres of writing, especially the ones I say I do not like such as poetry or science fiction. I promise to not get hung up on spelling - I can always look up words later, which I also promise to do.

I promise to share my writing, whether I share with just one person or a group of people. Sharing can be one word, one sentence, or an entire page of words. Although sharing may be uncomfortable for me, I recognise that whenever I share my thinking I am contributing to my writing community and that any contribution I make is greater than any fear I may have about my writing. I promise to quiet the censor in my head that says my writing is no good. *Writer woundedness*, therefore, ends with me. I promise to trust that I do have something to say. I promise to be kind to myself with first draft writing. I promise not to measure my writing against someone else's.

Above all, I promise to write as long as human thought is still valued and there are still words to be shared.

NOTE

[1] The Writing Promise was heavily inspired by Alice Ozma's The Reading Promise (p. 271) and includes some of her original lines as they speak to writing as much as reading. I encourage everyone to read The Reading Promise.

REFERENCE

Ozma, A. (2011). *The reading promise: My father and the books we shared.* New York, NY: Grand Central Publishing.

WORD WELL

Poppy Love	Departed Fizz	Lampin'
Star Sprink	Downshire Hill	Winter Torn
Sunset Stream	Under Construction	Olive Suffering
Moonbeam Wonderful	Peppered Heart	Poured Whole
Wayward Will	Stopless Cool	Sizzling Stars
Crumbling Bliss	Footprint	Leaf Bark
Jagged Pear	Prayer Twist	Vaulted Root
Cracked Whisper	Droplet Light	Culpable Dreams
Gentle Blind	Chizzil, Yo	Drifting Bruise
Heirloom Blessing	Great Things	Imperial Secret
Funnelled Stone	Passing Pulses	Whirring Jealous
Patriot Ode	Tropic Snow	Trip Up Foe
Noon's Blush	Suuweeet	Orbit Wish
Faith Faints	Blinking Hope	Flattened Breeze
Sun Wash	Trundled	Glistening Rage
Truethat	Candlelight Promises	Warm Shadow
Vomititious	Simmering Sadness	Together Thrown
Wide Wandering	Evergreen Long	Forest Tears
Viscous Tidings	Magenta Twinkle	Soft Death
Silver Shred	Willow Walk	Straightaway Joy
Warp Drive	Foxglove's Door	Tight Breathing
Sunlit Torches	Crescent Warrior	Wrinkled Pebble
Compass Star	Lady Moon	Porcelain Crag

NAMASTE FOR WRITERS

When we have finished our free-writes for the day, I invite students to say the words, "let it out, let it go, dissolve, reveal," in unison with me. Read together, these words speak to me as a kind of Namaste because they release the writer from writer woundedness by respecting the work that was done to unravel old writing wounds. The rhythm of these words as well as the repetition of the "l" sound in all four words appeals to me. There is also a level of vulnerability to the word dissolve. I like the idea of letting something out, letting it go, and letting it dissolve. Anything that we can reveal about ourselves on paper, whether it is a little or a lot, allows us to begin again. Ending *Namaste for Writers* with the word reveal, then, seems fitting.

let it out

let it go

dissolve

reveal